TEACHER'S PET PUBLICATIONS

PUZZLE PACK
for
Mythology

based on the book by
Edith Hamilton

Written by
William T. Collins

© 2005 Teacher's Pet Publications
All Rights Reserved

The materials in this packet are copyrighted
by Teacher's Pet Publications, Inc.

These pages may be duplicated by the purchaser
for use in the purchaser's own classroom.

Copying any of these materials and distributing them
for any other purpose is a violation of the copyright laws.

© 2005 Teacher's Pet Publications, Inc.
www.tpet.com

INTRODUCTION
If you already own the LitPlan for this title, this Puzzle Pack will refresh your Unit Resource Materials and Vocabulary Resource Materials sections plus give you additional materials you can substitute into the tests. If you do not already have a complete LitPlan, these pages will give you some supplemental materials to use with your own plan. There are two main groups of materials: one set for unit words (such as characters' names, symbols, places, etc.) and one set for vocabulary words associated with the book.

WORD LIST
There is a word list for both the unit words and the vocabulary words. These lists show you which words are being used in the materials and the clues or definitions being used for those words. You may want to give students a word list with clues/definitions to help them, or you may want students to only have a word list (without clues/definitions) if you want them to work a little harder. Both are available for duplication. The word lists can also be your "calling key" for the bingo games.

FILL IN THE BLANK AND MATCHING
There are 4 each of the fill in the blank and matching worksheets for both the unit and vocabulary words. These pages can be used either as extra worksheets for students or as objective parts of a unit test. They can be done individually if students need extra help or as a whole class activity to review the material covered.

MAGIC SQUARES
The magic squares not only reinforce the material covered but also work on reasoning and math skills. Many teachers have told us that their students really enjoy doing these!

WORD SEARCH PUZZLES
The word search words go in all directions, as indicated on your answer keys. Two of the word search puzzles have the clues listed rather than the words. This makes the puzzle a little more difficult, but it reinforces the material better. Two word search puzzles have words only for students who find the clue puzzles too difficult.

CROSSWORD PUZZLES
Both unit and vocabulary word sections have 4 crossword puzzles.

BINGO CARDS
There are 32 individual bingo cards for the unit words and 32 individual bingo cards for the vocabulary words. You can use your word list as a "call list," calling the words at random and marking them off of your list as you go, or you could use the flash cards by cutting them apart and drawing the words at random from a hat (or box or whatever). To make a better review, you might ask for the definition and spelling of each word as you call it out–or you could call out the definitions and have students tell you the words they need to look for on the puzzle.

JUGGLE LETTERS
The vocabulary juggle letter game is intended to help students learn the spellings of the words. One sheet has the definitions listed on it as an extra help for students who need it or to reinforce the definitions if you choose to do so.

FLASH CARDS
We've included a set of vocabulary flash cards you can duplicate, cut, and fold for your students. Some teachers make a few sets for general use by the class; others make a set for each student. Some teachers duplicate them for each student and have the students cut & fold their own. You can cut out just the words and put them in a hat, have each student pick out one word and write the definition and a sentence for that word. Students then swap words and papers, with the next student adding a sentence of his own under the last one. You can have students swap as many times as you like. Each time the student will read the sentences written prior to his own and then add a sentence. You can cut out the words and definitions separately and play "I Have; Who Has?" Each student in the room draws a word and definition. The first student says, "I have (the name of the word). Who has the definition?" The student with the definition reads it then says, "I have (the name of the vocabulary word she has). Who has the definition?" The round continues until all words and definitions have been given.

Mythology Word List

No.	Word	Clue/Definition
1.	ACHILLES	Had a vulnerable heel
2.	ADONIS	Loved by Persephone and Aphrodite
3.	AENEAS	Founder of the Roman race
4.	AGAMEMNON	Sacrificed his daughter
5.	AMAZONS	Warrior daughters of Harmony and Ares
6.	ANTIGONE	Buried her dead brother
7.	ARACHNE	Weaver turned into a spider
8.	ARIADNE	Helped Theseus escape from Labyrinth
9.	ASGARD	Home of Norse gods
10.	ATALANTA	Married winner of footrace
11.	ATHENA	Sprang full-grown from Zeus' head
12.	BACCHUS	Another name for Dionysus
13.	BELLEROPHON	Rode Pegasus to kill Chimaera
14.	BRYNHILD	Put to sleep as a punishment
15.	CALLISTO	Put in the sky as the Great Bear constellation
16.	CERBERUS	Guard-dog of the Underworld
17.	CHAOS	Immeasurable abyss at the beginning of everything
18.	CHIRON	Centaur who trained sons of heroes
19.	CRONUS	Titan father of Zeus
20.	CYCLOPS	One-eyed monster
21.	DAEDALUS	Creator of Labyrinth
22.	DELPHI	Location of Apollo's oracle
23.	DEMETER	Goddess of the Corn
24.	DIANA	Artemis, the Chief Huntsman
25.	DIDO	Founded Carthage
26.	DIONYSUS	God of Wine
27.	ELYSIAN	____Fields; place of blessedness where good was rewarded
28.	FLEECE	Golden ____ was the object of Jason's quest
29.	FREYA	Norse goddess of Love and Beauty
30.	FRIGGA	Wife of Odin
31.	GUNDRUN	Married Sigurd
32.	GUNNAR	His brother killed Sigurd
33.	HECTOR	Killed in battle with Achilles
34.	HELA	Ruler of Niflheim
35.	HELEN	Wife of Menelaus, kidnapped by Paris
36.	HEPHAESTUS	Vulcan, God of Fire
37.	HERA	Wife of Zeus, Protector of Marriage
38.	HERCULES	Performed twelve labors as a penance
39.	HERMES	Mercury, winged messenger of the gods
40.	HESTIA	Vesta, Goddess of the Hearth
41.	HOMER	Author of the Iliad and Odyssey
42.	ICARUS	Glue on his wings melted when he flew too close to the sun
43.	ILIAD	First written record of Greece
44.	IPHIGENIA	Sacrificed by Agamemnon for strong winds
45.	JASON	First hero in Europe who undertook a great journey
46.	LABYRINTH	Prison for Minotaur
47.	MEDEA	Helped Jason
48.	MENELAUS	Husband of Helen
49.	MIDAS	Wished for golden touch
50.	MIDGARD	Battlefield for men after death
51.	MINOTAUR	Half bull, half human

Copyrighted

Mythology Word List Continued

No.	Word	Clue/Definition
52.	NARCISSUS	Fell in love with his reflection in a pool
53.	NIFLHEIM	Norse Underworld
54.	ODIN	Solemn, aloof god
55.	ODYSSEUS	Had ten year journey after Trojan War
56.	OEDIPUS	Killed his father and married his mother
57.	ORION	Hunter placed in sky as a constellation
58.	PANDORA	Opened box of harmful things
59.	PARIS	Kidnapped Helen
60.	PEGASUS	Winged horse
61.	PENELOPE	Faithful wife of Odysseus
62.	PERSEPHONE	Lived on Earth and in Underworld
63.	PHILOMELA	Wove her story into a tapestry
64.	PLEIADES	Seven daughters of Atlas
65.	POLYNEICES	Creon refused him burial
66.	POSEIDON	Neptune, God of the Sea
67.	PROCNE	Changed into a nightingale
68.	PROMETHEUS	Gave man the gift of fire
69.	PSYCHE	Married Cupid
70.	PYGMALION	Fell in love with a statue
71.	RHEA	Mother of Zeus
72.	SIGMUND	Killed his sister's husband and children
73.	SISYPHUS	Rolled a rock forever uphill
74.	TANTALUS	Couldn't reach food or drink
75.	TELEMACHUS	Son of Odysseus
76.	THEOGONY	Account of the creation of the universe and the gods
77.	THESEUS	Made Athens a commonwealth
78.	THOR	God of Thunder
79.	TITANS	Elder Gods
80.	TROY	Besieged city
81.	TYR	Tuesday was named for him
82.	VALHALLA	Hall of the Slain
83.	WOODEN	____ horse; Greeks hid in it to enter Troy
84.	YMIR	Killed by Odin
85.	ZEUS	Jupiter, Cheif God

Mythology Fill In The Blanks 1

_____ 1. Killed his father and married his mother
_____ 2. Married Sigurd
_____ 3. Made Athens a commonwealth
_____ 4. Winged horse
_____ 5. Account of the creation of the universe and the gods
_____ 6. Sacrificed by Agamemnon for strong winds
_____ 7. Prison for Minotaur
_____ 8. Fell in love with a statue
_____ 9. Tuesday was named for him
_____ 10. Changed into a nightingale
_____ 11. Author of the Iliad and Odyssey
_____ 12. Elder Gods
_____ 13. Son of Odysseus
_____ 14. Centaur who trained sons of heroes
_____ 15. Besieged city
_____ 16. ____Fields; place of blessedness where good was rewarded
_____ 17. Ruler of Niflheim
_____ 18. ____horse; Greeks hid in it to enter Troy
_____ 19. Had ten year journey after Trojan War
_____ 20. First hero in Europe who undertook a great journey

Mythology Fill In The Blanks 1 Answer Key

OEDIPUS	1. Killed his father and married his mother
GUNDRUN	2. Married Sigurd
THESEUS	3. Made Athens a commonwealth
PEGASUS	4. Winged horse
THEOGONY	5. Account of the creation of the universe and the gods
IPHIGENIA	6. Sacrificed by Agamemnon for strong winds
LABYRINTH	7. Prison for Minotaur
PYGMALION	8. Fell in love with a statue
TYR	9. Tuesday was named for him
PROCNE	10. Changed into a nightingale
HOMER	11. Author of the Iliad and Odyssey
TITANS	12. Elder Gods
TELEMACHUS	13. Son of Odysseus
CHIRON	14. Centaur who trained sons of heroes
TROY	15. Besieged city
ELYSIAN	16. ____Fields; place of blessedness where good was rewarded
HELA	17. Ruler of Niflheim
WOODEN	18. ____horse; Greeks hid in it to enter Troy
ODYSSEUS	19. Had ten year journey after Trojan War
JASON	20. First hero in Europe who undertook a great journey

Mythology Fill In The Blanks 2

_____ 1. Jupiter, Cheif God
_____ 2. Rolled a rock forever uphill
_____ 3. His brother killed Sigurd
_____ 4. God of Wine
_____ 5. Killed in battle with Achilles
_____ 6. Wife of Zeus, Protector of Marriage
_____ 7. Artemis, the Chief Huntsman
_____ 8. Fell in love with a statue
_____ 9. Helped Theseus escape from Labyrinth
_____ 10. Married Cupid
_____ 11. Had ten year journey after Trojan War
_____ 12. Kidnapped Helen
_____ 13. Author of the Iliad and Odyssey
_____ 14. First written record of Greece
_____ 15. Golden ____ was the object of Jason's quest
_____ 16. Helped Jason
_____ 17. Sacrificed his daughter
_____ 18. Besieged city
_____ 19. Another name for Dionysus
_____ 20. Husband of Helen

Mythology Fill In The Blanks 2 Answer Key

ZEUS	1. Jupiter, Cheif God
SISYPHUS	2. Rolled a rock forever uphill
GUNNAR	3. His brother killed Sigurd
DIONYSUS	4. God of Wine
HECTOR	5. Killed in battle with Achilles
HERA	6. Wife of Zeus, Protector of Marriage
DIANA	7. Artemis, the Chief Huntsman
PYGMALION	8. Fell in love with a statue
ARIADNE	9. Helped Theseus escape from Labyrinth
PSYCHE	10. Married Cupid
ODYSSEUS	11. Had ten year journey after Trojan War
PARIS	12. Kidnapped Helen
HOMER	13. Author of the Iliad and Odyssey
ILIAD	14. First written record of Greece
FLEECE	15. Golden ____ was the object of Jason's quest
MEDEA	16. Helped Jason
AGAMEMNON	17. Sacrificed his daughter
TROY	18. Besieged city
BACCHUS	19. Another name for Dionysus
MENELAUS	20. Husband of Helen

Mythology Fill In The Blanks 3

_____ 1. Mercury, winged messenger of the gods
_____ 2. ____horse; Greeks hid in it to enter Troy
_____ 3. Norse goddess of Love and Beauty
_____ 4. Put to sleep as a punishment
_____ 5. Sprang full-grown from Zeus' head
_____ 6. Killed his father and married his mother
_____ 7. Kidnapped Helen
_____ 8. Rolled a rock forever uphill
_____ 9. Hall of the Slain
_____ 10. Account of the creation of the universe and the gods
_____ 11. ____Fields; place of blessedness where good was rewarded
_____ 12. Faithful wife of Odysseus
_____ 13. Mother of Zeus
_____ 14. Glue on his wings melted when he flew too close to the sun
_____ 15. Fell in love with his reflection in a pool
_____ 16. Seven daughters of Atlas
_____ 17. Solemn, aloof god
_____ 18. Goddess of the Corn
_____ 19. Founder of the Roman race
_____ 20. Wished for golden touch

Mythology Fill In The Blanks 3 Answer Key

HERMES	1. Mercury, winged messenger of the gods
WOODEN	2. ____horse; Greeks hid in it to enter Troy
FREYA	3. Norse goddess of Love and Beauty
BRYNHILD	4. Put to sleep as a punishment
ATHENA	5. Sprang full-grown from Zeus' head
OEDIPUS	6. Killed his father and married his mother
PARIS	7. Kidnapped Helen
SISYPHUS	8. Rolled a rock forever uphill
VALHALLA	9. Hall of the Slain
THEOGONY	10. Account of the creation of the universe and the gods
ELYSIAN	11. ____Fields; place of blessedness where good was rewarded
PENELOPE	12. Faithful wife of Odysseus
RHEA	13. Mother of Zeus
ICARUS	14. Glue on his wings melted when he flew too close to the sun
NARCISSUS	15. Fell in love with his reflection in a pool
PLEIADES	16. Seven daughters of Atlas
ODIN	17. Solemn, aloof god
DEMETER	18. Goddess of the Corn
AENEAS	19. Founder of the Roman race
MIDAS	20. Wished for golden touch

Mythology Fill In The Blanks 4

_____ 1. Faithful wife of Odysseus

_____ 2. Location of Apollo's oracle

_____ 3. Author of the Iliad and Odyssey

_____ 4. Sprang full-grown from Zeus' head

_____ 5. Wife of Menelaus, kidnapped by Paris

_____ 6. Norse Underworld

_____ 7. Killed in battle with Achilles

_____ 8. Had a vulnerable heel

_____ 9. Killed by Odin

_____ 10. His brother killed Sigurd

_____ 11. Goddess of the Corn

_____ 12. Gave man the gift of fire

_____ 13. God of Wine

_____ 14. ____Fields; place of blessedness where good was rewarded

_____ 15. Guard-dog of the Underworld

_____ 16. Ruler of Niflheim

_____ 17. Rode Pegasus to kill Chimaera

_____ 18. Married Sigurd

_____ 19. Buried her dead brother

_____ 20. Elder Gods

Mythology Fill In The Blanks 4 Answer Key

PENELOPE	1. Faithful wife of Odysseus
DELPHI	2. Location of Apollo's oracle
HOMER	3. Author of the Iliad and Odyssey
ATHENA	4. Sprang full-grown from Zeus' head
HELEN	5. Wife of Menelaus, kidnapped by Paris
NIFLHEIM	6. Norse Underworld
HECTOR	7. Killed in battle with Achilles
ACHILLES	8. Had a vulnerable heel
YMIR	9. Killed by Odin
GUNNAR	10. His brother killed Sigurd
DEMETER	11. Goddess of the Corn
PROMETHEUS	12. Gave man the gift of fire
DIONYSUS	13. God of Wine
ELYSIAN	14. ____Fields; place of blessedness where good was rewarded
CERBERUS	15. Guard-dog of the Underworld
HELA	16. Ruler of Niflheim
BELLEROPHON	17. Rode Pegasus to kill Chimaera
GUNDRUN	18. Married Sigurd
ANTIGONE	19. Buried her dead brother
TITANS	20. Elder Gods

Mythology Matching 1

___ 1. TROY   A. Kidnapped Helen
___ 2. YMIR   B. Creator of Labyrinth
___ 3. PEGASUS   C. Creon refused him burial
___ 4. PYGMALION   D. Golden ____ was the object of Jason's quest
___ 5. FLEECE   E. Founder of the Roman race
___ 6. PARIS   F. Killed his sister's husband and children
___ 7. POLYNEICES   G. Made Athens a commonwealth
___ 8. PROCNE   H. Killed in battle with Achilles
___ 9. ATHENA   I. Home of Norse gods
___10. DAEDALUS   J. Another name for Dionysus
___11. THESEUS   K. Put to sleep as a punishment
___12. AENEAS   L. Changed into a nightingale
___13. SIGMUND   M. Killed by Odin
___14. BELLEROPHON   N. Hunter placed in sky as a constellation
___15. HECTOR   O. Rode Pegasus to kill Chimaera
___16. BACCHUS   P. Wove her story into a tapestry
___17. GUNNAR   Q. God of Wine
___18. ORION   R. His brother killed Sigurd
___19. ASGARD   S. ____Fields; place of blessedness where good was rewarded
___20. THOR   T. Fell in love with a statue
___21. ELYSIAN   U. Immeasurable abyss at the beginning of everything
___22. PHILOMELA   V. God of Thunder
___23. CHAOS   W. Besieged city
___24. DIONYSUS   X. Winged horse
___25. BRYNHILD   Y. Sprang full-grown from Zeus' head

Mythology Matching 1 Answer Key

W - 1. TROY		A. Kidnapped Helen
M - 2. YMIR		B. Creator of Labyrinth
X - 3. PEGASUS		C. Creon refused him burial
T - 4. PYGMALION		D. Golden ____ was the object of Jason's quest
D - 5. FLEECE		E. Founder of the Roman race
A - 6. PARIS		F. Killed his sister's husband and children
C - 7. POLYNEICES		G. Made Athens a commonwealth
L - 8. PROCNE		H. Killed in battle with Achilles
Y - 9. ATHENA		I. Home of Norse gods
B - 10. DAEDALUS		J. Another name for Dionysus
G - 11. THESEUS		K. Put to sleep as a punishment
E - 12. AENEAS		L. Changed into a nightingale
F - 13. SIGMUND		M. Killed by Odin
O - 14. BELLEROPHON		N. Hunter placed in sky as a constellation
H - 15. HECTOR		O. Rode Pegasus to kill Chimaera
J - 16. BACCHUS		P. Wove her story into a tapestry
R - 17. GUNNAR		Q. God of Wine
N - 18. ORION		R. His brother killed Sigurd
I - 19. ASGARD		S. ____Fields; place of blessedness where good was rewarded
V - 20. THOR		T. Fell in love with a statue
S - 21. ELYSIAN		U. Immeasurable abyss at the beginning of everything
P - 22. PHILOMELA		V. God of Thunder
U - 23. CHAOS		W. Besieged city
Q - 24. DIONYSUS		X. Winged horse
K - 25. BRYNHILD		Y. Sprang full-grown from Zeus' head

Mythology Matching 2

___ 1. DIANA   A. Helped Theseus escape from Labyrinth
___ 2. HESTIA   B. Mother of Zeus
___ 3. SISYPHUS   C. Jupiter, Cheif God
___ 4. HELA   D. Sprang full-grown from Zeus' head
___ 5. RHEA   E. Vesta, Goddess of the Hearth
___ 6. BELLEROPHON   F. Home of Norse gods
___ 7. AENEAS   G. Ruler of Niflheim
___ 8. TELEMACHUS   H. Vulcan, God of Fire
___ 9. CYCLOPS   I. One-eyed monster
___10. HERMES   J. Fell in love with his reflection in a pool
___11. ZEUS   K. Rode Pegasus to kill Chimaera
___12. IPHIGENIA   L. Rolled a rock forever uphill
___13. MINOTAUR   M. Artemis, the Chief Huntsman
___14. PENELOPE   N. Titan father of Zeus
___15. ATHENA   O. Half bull, half human
___16. BACCHUS   P. Son of Odysseus
___17. CRONUS   Q. Founder of the Roman race
___18. HECTOR   R. Fell in love with a statue
___19. ACHILLES   S. Faithful wife of Odysseus
___20. ASGARD   T. Husband of Helen
___21. HEPHAESTUS   U. Had a vulnerable heel
___22. MENELAUS   V. Mercury, winged messenger of the gods
___23. ARIADNE   W. Another name for Dionysus
___24. PYGMALION   X. Sacrificed by Agamemnon for strong winds
___25. NARCISSUS   Y. Killed in battle with Achilles

Mythology Matching 2 Answer Key

- M - 1. DIANA
- E - 2. HESTIA
- L - 3. SISYPHUS
- G - 4. HELA
- B - 5. RHEA
- K - 6. BELLEROPHON
- Q - 7. AENEAS
- P - 8. TELEMACHUS
- I - 9. CYCLOPS
- V - 10. HERMES
- C - 11. ZEUS
- X - 12. IPHIGENIA
- O - 13. MINOTAUR
- S - 14. PENELOPE
- D - 15. ATHENA
- W - 16. BACCHUS
- N - 17. CRONUS
- Y - 18. HECTOR
- U - 19. ACHILLES
- F - 20. ASGARD
- H - 21. HEPHAESTUS
- T - 22. MENELAUS
- A - 23. ARIADNE
- R - 24. PYGMALION
- J - 25. NARCISSUS

A. Helped Theseus escape from Labyrinth
B. Mother of Zeus
C. Jupiter, Cheif God
D. Sprang full-grown from Zeus' head
E. Vesta, Goddess of the Hearth
F. Home of Norse gods
G. Ruler of Niflheim
H. Vulcan, God of Fire
I. One-eyed monster
J. Fell in love with his reflection in a pool
K. Rode Pegasus to kill Chimaera
L. Rolled a rock forever uphill
M. Artemis, the Chief Huntsman
N. Titan father of Zeus
O. Half bull, half human
P. Son of Odysseus
Q. Founder of the Roman race
R. Fell in love with a statue
S. Faithful wife of Odysseus
T. Husband of Helen
U. Had a vulnerable heel
V. Mercury, winged messenger of the gods
W. Another name for Dionysus
X. Sacrificed by Agamemnon for strong winds
Y. Killed in battle with Achilles

Mythology Matching 3

___ 1. SISYPHUS   A. Another name for Dionysus
___ 2. LABYRINTH   B. Rolled a rock forever uphill
___ 3. BACCHUS   C. Neptune, God of the Sea
___ 4. TITANS   D. Location of Apollo's oracle
___ 5. JASON   E. Loved by Persephone and Aphrodite
___ 6. POSEIDON   F. Author of the Iliad and Odyssey
___ 7. HOMER   G. Besieged city
___ 8. DELPHI   H. Wished for golden touch
___ 9. TANTALUS   I. Sprang full-grown from Zeus' head
___10. TROY   J. Founder of the Roman race
___11. DEMETER   K. Guard-dog of the Underworld
___12. HERA   L. Gave man the gift of fire
___13. VALHALLA   M. Hall of the Slain
___14. PROMETHEUS   N. Warrior daughters of Harmony and Ares
___15. ADONIS   O. Wife of Zeus, Protector of Marriage
___16. AMAZONS   P. First hero in Europe who undertook a great journey
___17. CERBERUS   Q. Couldn't reach food or drink
___18. MIDAS   R. Hunter placed in sky as a constellation
___19. ORION   S. Opened box of harmful things
___20. TELEMACHUS   T. Elder Gods
___21. PSYCHE   U. Prison for Minotaur
___22. ZEUS   V. Married Cupid
___23. PANDORA   W. Jupiter, Cheif God
___24. ATHENA   X. Goddess of the Corn
___25. AENEAS   Y. Son of Odysseus

Mythology Matching 3 Answer Key

B - 1.	SISYPHUS	A.	Another name for Dionysus
U - 2.	LABYRINTH	B.	Rolled a rock forever uphill
A - 3.	BACCHUS	C.	Neptune, God of the Sea
T - 4.	TITANS	D.	Location of Apollo's oracle
P - 5.	JASON	E.	Loved by Persephone and Aphrodite
C - 6.	POSEIDON	F.	Author of the Iliad and Odyssey
F - 7.	HOMER	G.	Besieged city
D - 8.	DELPHI	H.	Wished for golden touch
Q - 9.	TANTALUS	I.	Sprang full-grown from Zeus' head
G -10.	TROY	J.	Founder of the Roman race
X -11.	DEMETER	K.	Guard-dog of the Underworld
O -12.	HERA	L.	Gave man the gift of fire
M -13.	VALHALLA	M.	Hall of the Slain
L -14.	PROMETHEUS	N.	Warrior daughters of Harmony and Ares
E -15.	ADONIS	O.	Wife of Zeus, Protector of Marriage
N -16.	AMAZONS	P.	First hero in Europe who undertook a great journey
K -17.	CERBERUS	Q.	Couldn't reach food or drink
H -18.	MIDAS	R.	Hunter placed in sky as a constellation
R -19.	ORION	S.	Opened box of harmful things
Y -20.	TELEMACHUS	T.	Elder Gods
V -21.	PSYCHE	U.	Prison for Minotaur
W -22.	ZEUS	V.	Married Cupid
S -23.	PANDORA	W.	Jupiter, Cheif God
I - 24.	ATHENA	X.	Goddess of the Corn
J - 25.	AENEAS	Y.	Son of Odysseus

Mythology Matching 4

___ 1. CRONUS   A. Half bull, half human
___ 2. ADONIS   B. Winged horse
___ 3. HESTIA   C. Helped Theseus escape from Labyrinth
___ 4. THEOGONY   D. Helped Jason
___ 5. PSYCHE   E. Account of the creation of the universe and the gods
___ 6. YMIR   F. Killed by Odin
___ 7. IPHIGENIA   G. One-eyed monster
___ 8. PEGASUS   H. Titan father of Zeus
___ 9. GUNNAR   I. Married Cupid
___10. THESEUS   J. Norse goddess of Love and Beauty
___11. SISYPHUS   K. His brother killed Sigurd
___12. ARIADNE   L. Had ten year journey after Trojan War
___13. ELYSIAN   M. ____Fields; place of blessedness where good was rewarded
___14. JASON   N. Sacrificed by Agamemnon for strong winds
___15. MEDEA   O. Gave man the gift of fire
___16. FLEECE   P. Artemis, the Chief Huntsman
___17. MINOTAUR   Q. Loved by Persephone and Aphrodite
___18. DIANA   R. Vesta, Goddess of the Hearth
___19. PROMETHEUS   S. Rolled a rock forever uphill
___20. FREYA   T. First hero in Europe who undertook a great journey
___21. PYGMALION   U. Made Athens a commonwealth
___22. OEDIPUS   V. Killed his father and married his mother
___23. CYCLOPS   W. Author of the Iliad and Odyssey
___24. HOMER   X. Golden ____ was the object of Jason's quest
___25. ODYSSEUS   Y. Fell in love with a statue

Mythology Matching 4 Answer Key

H - 1. CRONUS	A.	Half bull, half human
Q - 2. ADONIS	B.	Winged horse
R - 3. HESTIA	C.	Helped Theseus escape from Labyrinth
E - 4. THEOGONY	D.	Helped Jason
I - 5. PSYCHE	E.	Account of the creation of the universe and the gods
F - 6. YMIR	F.	Killed by Odin
N - 7. IPHIGENIA	G.	One-eyed monster
B - 8. PEGASUS	H.	Titan father of Zeus
K - 9. GUNNAR	I.	Married Cupid
U -10. THESEUS	J.	Norse goddess of Love and Beauty
S -11. SISYPHUS	K.	His brother killed Sigurd
C -12. ARIADNE	L.	Had ten year journey after Trojan War
M -13. ELYSIAN	M.	____Fields; place of blessedness where good was rewarded
T -14. JASON	N.	Sacrificed by Agamemnon for strong winds
D -15. MEDEA	O.	Gave man the gift of fire
X -16. FLEECE	P.	Artemis, the Chief Huntsman
A -17. MINOTAUR	Q.	Loved by Persephone and Aphrodite
P -18. DIANA	R.	Vesta, Goddess of the Hearth
O -19. PROMETHEUS	S.	Rolled a rock forever uphill
J -20. FREYA	T.	First hero in Europe who undertook a great journey
Y -21. PYGMALION	U.	Made Athens a commonwealth
V -22. OEDIPUS	V.	Killed his father and married his mother
G -23. CYCLOPS	W.	Author of the Iliad and Odyssey
W -24. HOMER	X.	Golden ____ was the object of Jason's quest
L -25. ODYSSEUS	Y.	Fell in love with a statue

Mythology Magic Squares 1

Match the definition with the vocabulary word. Put your answers in the magic squares below. When your answers are correct, all columns and rows will add to the same number.

A. NARCISSUS   G. TANTALUS   M. DIDO
B. PHILOMELA   H. CRONUS   N. HESTIA
C. POLYNEICES   I. BELLEROPHON   O. PLEIADES
D. ODYSSEUS   J. SIGMUND   P. PENELOPE
E. ORION   K. ATALANTA
F. YMIR   L. CYCLOPS

1. Titan father of Zeus
2. Fell in love with his reflection in a pool
3. Wove her story into a tapestry
4. Couldn't reach food or drink
5. Killed his sister's husband and children
6. Seven daughters of Atlas
7. Faithful wife of Odysseus
8. Rode Pegasus to kill Chimaera
9. Married winner of footrace
10. Vesta, Goddess of the Hearth
11. Founded Carthage
12. One-eyed monster
13. Hunter placed in sky as a constellation
14. Had ten year journey after Trojan War
15. Creon refused him burial
16. Killed by Odin

A=	B=	C=	D=
E=	F=	G=	H=
I=	J=	K=	L=
M=	N=	O=	P=

Mythology Magic Squares 1 Answer Key

Match the definition with the vocabulary word. Put your answers in the magic squares below. When your answers are correct, all columns and rows will add to the same number.

- A. NARCISSUS
- B. PHILOMELA
- C. POLYNEICES
- D. ODYSSEUS
- E. ORION
- F. YMIR
- G. TANTALUS
- H. CRONUS
- I. BELLEROPHON
- J. SIGMUND
- K. ATALANTA
- L. CYCLOPS
- M. DIDO
- N. HESTIA
- O. PLEIADES
- P. PENELOPE

1. Titan father of Zeus
2. Fell in love with his reflection in a pool
3. Wove her story into a tapestry
4. Couldn't reach food or drink
5. Killed his sister's husband and children
6. Seven daughters of Atlas
7. Faithful wife of Odysseus
8. Rode Pegasus to kill Chimaera
9. Married winner of footrace
10. Vesta, Goddess of the Hearth
11. Founded Carthage
12. One-eyed monster
13. Hunter placed in sky as a constellation
14. Had ten year journey after Trojan War
15. Creon refused him burial
16. Killed by Odin

A=2	B=3	C=15	D=14
E=13	F=16	G=4	H=1
I=8	J=5	K=9	L=12
M=11	N=10	O=6	P=7

Mythology Magic Squares 2

Match the definition with the vocabulary word. Put your answers in the magic squares below. When your answers are correct, all columns and rows will add to the same number.

A. ATHENA
B. HERCULES
C. GUNDRUN
D. ARIADNE
E. SIGMUND
F. AENEAS
G. DIANA
H. NARCISSUS
I. NIFLHEIM
J. ADONIS
K. HELEN
L. ZEUS
M. THEOGONY
N. THESEUS
O. POLYNEICES
P. HERMES

1. Creon refused him burial
2. Helped Theseus escape from Labyrinth
3. Loved by Persephone and Aphrodite
4. Killed his sister's husband and children
5. Norse Underworld
6. Founder of the Roman race
7. Mercury, winged messenger of the gods
8. Married Sigurd
9. Fell in love with his reflection in a pool
10. Wife of Menelaus, kidnapped by Paris
11. Sprang full-grown from Zeus' head
12. Made Athens a commonwealth
13. Performed twelve labors as a penance
14. Account of the creation of the universe and the gods
15. Artemis, the Chief Huntsman
16. Jupiter, Cheif God

A=	B=	C=	D=
E=	F=	G=	H=
I=	J=	K=	L=
M=	N=	O=	P=

Mythology Magic Squares 2 Answer Key

Match the definition with the vocabulary word. Put your answers in the magic squares below. When your answers are correct, all columns and rows will add to the same number.

A. ATHENA
B. HERCULES
C. GUNDRUN
D. ARIADNE
E. SIGMUND
F. AENEAS
G. DIANA
H. NARCISSUS
I. NIFLHEIM
J. ADONIS
K. HELEN
L. ZEUS
M. THEOGONY
N. THESEUS
O. POLYNEICES
P. HERMES

1. Creon refused him burial
2. Helped Theseus escape from Labyrinth
3. Loved by Persephone and Aphrodite
4. Killed his sister's husband and children
5. Norse Underworld
6. Founder of the Roman race
7. Mercury, winged messenger of the gods
8. Married Sigurd
9. Fell in love with his reflection in a pool
10. Wife of Menelaus, kidnapped by Paris
11. Sprang full-grown from Zeus' head
12. Made Athens a commonwealth
13. Performed twelve labors as a penance
14. Account of the creation of the universe and the gods
15. Artemis, the Chief Huntsman
16. Jupiter, Cheif God

A=11	B=13	C=8	D=2
E=4	F=6	G=15	H=9
I=5	J=3	K=10	L=16
M=14	N=12	O=1	P=7

Mythology Magic Squares 3

Match the definition with the vocabulary word. Put your answers in the magic squares below. When your answers are correct, all columns and rows will add to the same number.

A. ARIADNE
B. PLEIADES
C. WOODEN
D. BACCHUS
E. BELLEROPHON
F. PYGMALION
G. CERBERUS
H. ODYSSEUS
I. HOMER
J. GUNDRUN
K. ARACHNE
L. CRONUS
M. AENEAS
N. CHIRON
O. DIANA
P. PROCNE

1. Had ten year journey after Trojan War
2. Founder of the Roman race
3. Seven daughters of Atlas
4. Weaver turned into a spider
5. Married Sigurd
6. ____ horse; Greeks hid in it to enter Troy
7. Changed into a nightingale
8. Rode Pegasus to kill Chimaera
9. Artemis, the Chief Huntsman
10. Fell in love with a statue
11. Author of the Iliad and Odyssey
12. Another name for Dionysus
13. Helped Theseus escape from Labyrinth
14. Titan father of Zeus
15. Guard-dog of the Underworld
16. Centaur who trained sons of heroes

A=	B=	C=	D=
E=	F=	G=	H=
I=	J=	K=	L=
M=	N=	O=	P=

Mythology Magic Squares 3 Answer Key

Match the definition with the vocabulary word. Put your answers in the magic squares below. When your answers are correct, all columns and rows will add to the same number.

A. ARIADNE
B. PLEIADES
C. WOODEN
D. BACCHUS
E. BELLEROPHON
F. PYGMALION
G. CERBERUS
H. ODYSSEUS
I. HOMER
J. GUNDRUN
K. ARACHNE
L. CRONUS
M. AENEAS
N. CHIRON
O. DIANA
P. PROCNE

1. Had ten year journey after Trojan War
2. Founder of the Roman race
3. Seven daughters of Atlas
4. Weaver turned into a spider
5. Married Sigurd
6. ____ horse; Greeks hid in it to enter Troy
7. Changed into a nightingale
8. Rode Pegasus to kill Chimaera
9. Artemis, the Chief Huntsman
10. Fell in love with a statue
11. Author of the Iliad and Odyssey
12. Another name for Dionysus
13. Helped Theseus escape from Labyrinth
14. Titan father of Zeus
15. Guard-dog of the Underworld
16. Centaur who trained sons of heroes

A=13	B=3	C=6	D=12
E=8	F=10	G=15	H=1
I=11	J=5	K=4	L=14
M=2	N=16	O=9	P=7

Mythology Magic Squares 4

Match the definition with the vocabulary word. Put your answers in the magic squares below. When your answers are correct, all columns and rows will add to the same number.

A. ODYSSEUS
B. MIDGARD
C. LABYRINTH
D. PYGMALION
E. PROCNE
F. THOR
G. NARCISSUS
H. HERMES
I. ARACHNE
J. ILIAD
K. ICARUS
L. NIFLHEIM
M. ODIN
N. ORION
O. CALLISTO
P. BACCHUS

1. Mercury, winged messenger of the gods
2. Solemn, aloof god
3. Battlefield for men after death
4. Glue on his wings melted when he flew too close to the sun
5. First written record of Greece
6. Prison for Minotaur
7. Another name for Dionysus
8. Changed into a nightingale
9. Put in the sky as the Great Bear constellation
10. God of Thunder
11. Weaver turned into a spider
12. Fell in love with a statue
13. Had ten year journey after Trojan War
14. Norse Underworld
15. Fell in love with his reflection in a pool
16. Hunter placed in sky as a constellation

A=	B=	C=	D=
E=	F=	G=	H=
I=	J=	K=	L=
M=	N=	O=	P=

Mythology Magic Squares 4 Answer Key

Match the definition with the vocabulary word. Put your answers in the magic squares below. When your answers are correct, all columns and rows will add to the same number.

A. ODYSSEUS
B. MIDGARD
C. LABYRINTH
D. PYGMALION
E. PROCNE
F. THOR
G. NARCISSUS
H. HERMES
I. ARACHNE
J. ILIAD
K. ICARUS
L. NIFLHEIM
M. ODIN
N. ORION
O. CALLISTO
P. BACCHUS

1. Mercury, winged messenger of the gods
2. Solemn, aloof god
3. Battlefield for men after death
4. Glue on his wings melted when he flew too close to the sun
5. First written record of Greece
6. Prison for Minotaur
7. Another name for Dionysus
8. Changed into a nightingale
9. Put in the sky as the Great Bear constellation
10. God of Thunder
11. Weaver turned into a spider
12. Fell in love with a statue
13. Had ten year journey after Trojan War
14. Norse Underworld
15. Fell in love with his reflection in a pool
16. Hunter placed in sky as a constellation

A=13	B=3	C=6	D=12
E=8	F=10	G=15	H=1
I=11	J=5	K=4	L=14
M=2	N=16	O=9	P=7

Mythology Word Search 1

```
C E R B E R U S U S A G E P Z D I A N A
S H F R E Y A A U N N P A M S F R E S X
U F A W X H I N K J O C L I U E N N V C
H L R O H T O Y S L H A X L H H A E H R
C E P H S R N M E I B N J I C E N A N K
A E L E C O Y N L Y S W Y A C R S S E T
M C H W G B E L R T S Y R D A C U K L X
E E D O V P E I A S D A P N B U R T Y Y
L X E E A S N K G J R W V H A L A H S D
E H W G L T J T A E C M X L U E C O I S
T R O Y H P R O M E T H E U S S I R A P
H Y D G A A H O E I G H S R E X I E N W
A P R U L T H I M J D P T M J M D F Q N
B S A N L H Z C N A B A R S Y E D R N W
W Y G N A E E Z O S K E S O M O D I N Y
H C D A X N U L N O H N P H C L C G D Q
D H I R R A S J E N P N U R D N U G Q O
V E M N E D O O W N A D O N I S E A B Y
```

Account of the creation of the universe and the gods (8)
Another name for Dionysus (7)
Artemis, the Chief Huntsman (5)
Author of the Iliad and Odyssey (5)
Battlefield for men after death (7)
Besieged city (4)
Changed into a nightingale (6)
Faithful wife of Odysseus (8)
First hero in Europe who undertook a great journey (5)
First written record of Greece (5)
Founded Carthage (4)
Founder of the Roman race (6)
Gave man the gift of fire (10)
Glue on his wings melted when he flew too close to the sun (6)
God of Thunder (4)
Golden ____ was the object of Jason's quest (6)
Guard-dog of the Underworld (8)
Had a vulnerable heel (8)
Hall of the Slain (8)
Helped Jason (5)
His brother killed Sigurd (6)
Home of Norse gods (6)
Immeasurable abyss at the beginning of everything (5)
Jupiter, Cheif God (4)
Kidnapped Helen (5)
Killed by Odin (4)

Location of Apollo's oracle (6)
Loved by Persephone and Aphrodite (6)
Married Cupid (6)
Married Sigurd (7)
Mercury, winged messenger of the gods (6)
Mother of Zeus (4)
Norse goddess of Love and Beauty (5)
Performed twelve labors as a penance (8)
Prison for Minotaur (9)
Rolled a rock forever uphill (8)
Ruler of Niflheim (4)
Sacrificed his daughter (9)
Solemn, aloof god (4)
Son of Odysseus (10)
Sprang full-grown from Zeus' head (6)
Titan father of Zeus (6)
Tuesday was named for him (3)
Vesta, Goddess of the Hearth (6)
Weaver turned into a spider (7)
Wife of Menelaus, kidnapped by Paris (5)
Wife of Odin (6)
Wife of Zeus, Protector of Marriage (4)
Winged horse (7)
Wished for golden touch (5)
____Fields; place of blessedness where good was rewarded (7)
____horse; Greeks hid in it to enter Troy (6)

Mythology Word Search 1 Answer Key

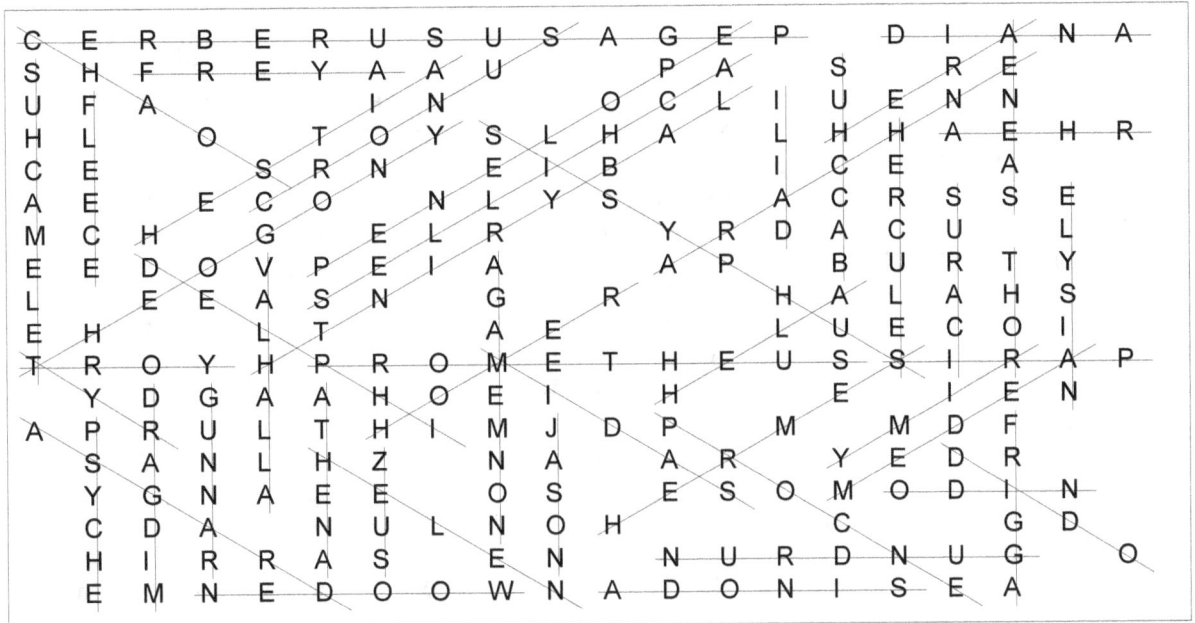

Account of the creation of the universe and the gods (8)
Another name for Dionysus (7)
Artemis, the Chief Huntsman (5)
Author of the Iliad and Odyssey (5)
Battlefield for men after death (7)
Besieged city (4)
Changed into a nightingale (6)
Faithful wife of Odysseus (8)
First hero in Europe who undertook a great journey (5)
First written record of Greece (5)
Founded Carthage (4)
Founder of the Roman race (6)
Gave man the gift of fire (10)
Glue on his wings melted when he flew too close to the sun (6)
God of Thunder (4)
Golden ____ was the object of Jason's quest (6)
Guard-dog of the Underworld (8)
Had a vulnerable heel (8)
Hall of the Slain (8)
Helped Jason (5)
His brother killed Sigurd (6)
Home of Norse gods (6)
Immeasurable abyss at the beginning of everything (5)
Jupiter, Cheif God (4)
Kidnapped Helen (5)
Killed by Odin (4)

Location of Apollo's oracle (6)
Loved by Persephone and Aphrodite (6)
Married Cupid (6)
Married Sigurd (7)
Mercury, winged messenger of the gods (6)
Mother of Zeus (4)
Norse goddess of Love and Beauty (5)
Performed twelve labors as a penance (8)
Prison for Minotaur (9)
Rolled a rock forever uphill (8)
Ruler of Niflheim (4)
Sacrificed his daughter (9)
Solemn, aloof god (4)
Son of Odysseus (10)
Sprang full-grown from Zeus' head (6)
Titan father of Zeus (6)
Tuesday was named for him (3)
Vesta, Goddess of the Hearth (6)
Weaver turned into a spider (7)
Wife of Menelaus, kidnapped by Paris (5)
Wife of Odin (6)
Wife of Zeus, Protector of Marriage (4)
Winged horse (7)
Wished for golden touch (5)
____Fields; place of blessedness where good was rewarded (7)
____horse; Greeks hid in it to enter Troy (6)

Mythology Word Search 2

```
C T H S D Z P A S A T H E N A H O M E R
G J T I C T Z T T I M T H R T G D R R L
R W A N N Y T N B R S Y E H A J O O K
B N F O O S C A Y B O Y I Z R E T H D R
A T Q D N O I L A M G Y P E Z C A T Y P
C E W A M A J A O N I S H H E C U T S Z
C L N F E H S T W P Y R I H U S D L S M
H E H E M C R A T C S B G K S S G S E V
U M E J A S O N H F L E E C E U P I U S
S A R N G S I E E E N L N G N P E G S J
M C M I A D F D O O L I N C I N M U P
I H E F O V P Q G H D E A C O D E U R Y
N U S L A N A I O E I R N R R E L N A L
O S T H S G T B N L D O O O P O O D C M
T W V E G N D V Y A O P I N H Q P Q I B
A I L I A D M I D A S H R U F R E Y A Q
U K R M R T I T A N S O O S H E S T I A
R F N E D O O W N P A N D O R A E D E M
```

Account of the creation of the universe and the gods (8)
Another name for Dionysus (7)
Artemis, the Chief Huntsman (5)
Author of the Iliad and Odyssey (5)
Besieged city (4)
Buried her dead brother (8)
Changed into a nightingale (6)
Elder Gods (6)
Faithful wife of Odysseus (8)
Fell in love with a statue (9)
First hero in Europe who undertook a great journey (5)
First written record of Greece (5)
Founded Carthage (4)
Founder of the Roman race (6)
Glue on his wings melted when he flew too close to the sun (6)
God of Thunder (4)
Golden ____ was the object of Jason's quest (6)
Had ten year journey after Trojan War (8)
Half bull, half human (8)
Helped Jason (5)
His brother killed Sigurd (6)
Home of Norse gods (6)
Hunter placed in sky as a constellation (5)
Immeasurable abyss at the beginning of everything (5)
Jupiter, Cheif God (4)
Killed by Odin (4)

Killed his father and married his mother (7)
Killed his sister's husband and children (7)
Killed in battle with Achilles (6)
Loved by Persephone and Aphrodite (6)
Married Cupid (6)
Married winner of footrace (8)
Mercury, winged messenger of the gods (6)
Mother of Zeus (4)
Norse Underworld (8)
Norse goddess of Love and Beauty (5)
One-eyed monster (7)
Opened box of harmful things (7)
Performed twelve labors as a penance (8)
Rode Pegasus to kill Chimaera (11)
Rolled a rock forever uphill (8)
Ruler of Niflheim (4)
Sacrificed by Agamemnon for strong winds (9)
Sacrificed his daughter (9)
Solemn, aloof god (4)
Son of Odysseus (10)
Sprang full-grown from Zeus' head (6)
Titan father of Zeus (6)
Tuesday was named for him (3)
Vesta, Goddess of the Hearth (6)
Wife of Menelaus, kidnapped by Paris (5)
Wife of Odin (6)
Wife of Zeus, Protector of Marriage (4)
Wished for golden touch (5)
____ horse; Greeks hid in it to enter Troy (6)

Mythology Word Search 2 Answer Key

Account of the creation of the universe and the gods (8)
Another name for Dionysus (7)
Artemis, the Chief Huntsman (5)
Author of the Iliad and Odyssey (5)
Besieged city (4)
Buried her dead brother (8)
Changed into a nightingale (6)
Elder Gods (6)
Faithful wife of Odysseus (8)
Fell in love with a statue (9)
First hero in Europe who undertook a great journey (5)
First written record of Greece (5)
Founded Carthage (4)
Founder of the Roman race (6)
Glue on his wings melted when he flew too close to the sun (6)
God of Thunder (4)
Golden ____ was the object of Jason's quest (6)
Had ten year journey after Trojan War (8)
Half bull, half human (8)
Helped Jason (5)
His brother killed Sigurd (6)
Home of Norse gods (6)
Hunter placed in sky as a constellation (5)
Immeasurable abyss at the beginning of everything (5)
Jupiter, Cheif God (4)
Killed by Odin (4)

Killed his father and married his mother (7)
Killed his sister's husband and children (7)
Killed in battle with Achilles (6)
Loved by Persephone and Aphrodite (6)
Married Cupid (6)
Married winner of footrace (8)
Mercury, winged messenger of the gods (6)
Mother of Zeus (4)
Norse Underworld (8)
Norse goddess of Love and Beauty (5)
One-eyed monster (7)
Opened box of harmful things (7)
Performed twelve labors as a penance (8)
Rode Pegasus to kill Chimaera (11)
Rolled a rock forever uphill (8)
Ruler of Niflheim (4)
Sacrificed by Agamemnon for strong winds (9)
Sacrificed his daughter (9)
Solemn, aloof god (4)
Son of Odysseus (10)
Sprang full-grown from Zeus' head (6)
Titan father of Zeus (6)
Tuesday was named for him (3)
Vesta, Goddess of the Hearth (6)
Wife of Menelaus, kidnapped by Paris (5)
Wife of Odin (6)
Wife of Zeus, Protector of Marriage (4)
Wished for golden touch (5)
____ horse; Greeks hid in it to enter Troy (6)

Mythology Word Search 3

```
V A L H A L L A B Y R I N T H D S S A X
K B Y N D C J S U H C C A B W U N G P
N Y V E O Y H W S A E N E A R A R S N
A R O D N A P I L M E R K E A I N Y X K
I A G O I P K E L H M S B C D U C Q E V
S N R O S R M Z T L I R I V R H B C C T
Y N E W M O O A L G E J T D E M E T R
L U M P L C D N M C P S N S R E L S G
E G O I L N I U V X E U T L L H U S Z
I P H I G E N I A G G I R F R H E A R
N P S E W D I K Q M A L H X X S R L U M
I W I F R E Y A D E S I H L E A O C E Q
F P S F M C L F D D U A T H C H P H S N
L T Y R Z E U S N E S D T H R D H A S Z
H C P G P Z G L N A S T N E O A O O Y J
E H H F M T G D E Z K E C R N R N S D Y
I I U V I A A R S S S O M M U E D H O B
M R S T N I L A S G A R D E S H E D M K
Y O A O R L R I S Q I I B S X C L I S
S N S A Z P R Z O M B O Z P T C P D D R
S A L E H A T L Y N K N Y O R T H O A T
J S Y S P O L C Y C G D R A G D I M S Z
```

ACHILLES	DIANA	ICARUS	PLEIADES
ADONIS	DIDO	ILIAD	PROCNE
AENEAS	ELYSIAN	IPHIGENIA	PSYCHE
ARACHNE	FLEECE	JASON	PYGMALION
ARIADNE	FREYA	LABYRINTH	RHEA
ASGARD	FRIGGA	MEDEA	SIGMUND
ATHENA	GUNDRUN	MIDAS	SISYPHUS
BACCHUS	GUNNAR	MIDGARD	THESEUS
BELLEROPHON	HECTOR	NIFLHEIM	THOR
CERBERUS	HELA	ODIN	TITANS
CHAOS	HELEN	ODYSSEUS	TROY
CHIRON	HERA	ORION	TYR
CRONUS	HERCULES	PANDORA	VALHALLA
CYCLOPS	HERMES	PARIS	WOODEN
DELPHI	HESTIA	PEGASUS	YMIR
DEMETER	HOMER	PHILOMELA	ZEUS

Mythology Word Search 3 Answer Key

ACHILLES	DIANA	ICARUS	PLEIADES
ADONIS	DIDO	ILIAD	PROCNE
AENEAS	ELYSIAN	IPHIGENIA	PSYCHE
ARACHNE	FLEECE	JASON	PYGMALION
ARIADNE	FREYA	LABYRINTH	RHEA
ASGARD	FRIGGA	MEDEA	SIGMUND
ATHENA	GUNDRUN	MIDAS	SISYPHUS
BACCHUS	GUNNAR	MIDGARD	THESEUS
BELLEROPHON	HECTOR	NIFLHEIM	THOR
CERBERUS	HELA	ODIN	TITANS
CHAOS	HELEN	ODYSSEUS	TROY
CHIRON	HERA	ORION	TYR
CRONUS	HERCULES	PANDORA	VALHALLA
CYCLOPS	HERMES	PARIS	WOODEN
DELPHI	HESTIA	PEGASUS	YMIR
DEMETER	HOMER	PHILOMELA	ZEUS

Mythology Word Search 4

```
A C R U A T O N I M P E N E L O P E T L
E S N X W G U N N R C J D H G E C H S D
N N G R P R A P P E J A E E U D R C O S
E S B A D H O M E S L R N I O O O G S J
A B K N R Q E L I T P C N P N R P N J Q
S Q U D Q D F R N M H U A U U S F Y Q W
O G F R E Y A O A Q I L R S S R R T Q
T Y P A P N D C T Z O E E F S N I J
S D P E T A N Y H V A N S L B N G T H
I E A M R O G C E D L I H N Y R B I G
L M N Y I S N L N S U Y K S P N G T G
L E D R A D E O A P S I G E I J H A B
A T O S L N A P O C O A N N A N B N J
C E R B E R U S H S H D I O N Y S U S F
D R A L H S E E H O A I Y C R U Z U M J
G R E L P I R D B I N R L S A M E Q F L
X H Y P D A P I R J O E C S S N S K N
J E Y O S U L A D E A D E Z E E T H O R
T A N M D Y X N R B Q N I H E S U R T N
Y J W N I S C A V I E C T N F U I S R G
R D I D O R C H M M S O A H C H S T O Y
W O O D E N T H E R M E S L C L Y K Y G
```

ACHILLES	CYCLOPS	HELA	ODYSSEUS	THEOGONY
ADONIS	DAEDALUS	HELEN	OEDIPUS	THESEUS
AENEAS	DELPHI	HERA	ORION	THOR
AGAMEMNON	DEMETER	HERCULES	PANDORA	TITANS
ARIADNE	DIANA	HERMES	PARIS	TROY
ASGARD	DIDO	HOMER	PENELOPE	TYR
ATHENA	DIONYSUS	ILIAD	PERSEPHONE	WOODEN
BRYNHILD	ELYSIAN	JASON	POSEIDON	YMIR
CALLISTO	FLEECE	MEDEA	PROCNE	ZEUS
CERBERUS	FREYA	MENELAUS	PSYCHE	
CHAOS	FRIGGA	MIDAS	RHEA	
CHIRON	GUNDRUN	MINOTAUR	SISYPHUS	
CRONUS	GUNNAR	ODIN	TANTALUS	

Mythology Word Search 4 Answer Key

ACHILLES	CYCLOPS	HELA	ODYSSEUS	THEOGONY
ADONIS	DAEDALUS	HELEN	OEDIPUS	THESEUS
AENEAS	DELPHI	HERA	ORION	THOR
AGAMEMNON	DEMETER	HERCULES	PANDORA	TITANS
ARIADNE	DIANA	HERMES	PARIS	TROY
ASGARD	DIDO	HOMER	PENELOPE	TYR
ATHENA	DIONYSUS	ILIAD	PERSEPHONE	WOODEN
BRYNHILD	ELYSIAN	JASON	POSEIDON	YMIR
CALLISTO	FLEECE	MEDEA	PROCNE	ZEUS
CERBERUS	FREYA	MENELAUS	PSYCHE	
CHAOS	FRIGGA	MIDAS	RHEA	
CHIRON	GUNDRUN	MINOTAUR	SISYPHUS	
CRONUS	GUNNAR	ODIN	TANTALUS	

Mythology Crossword 1

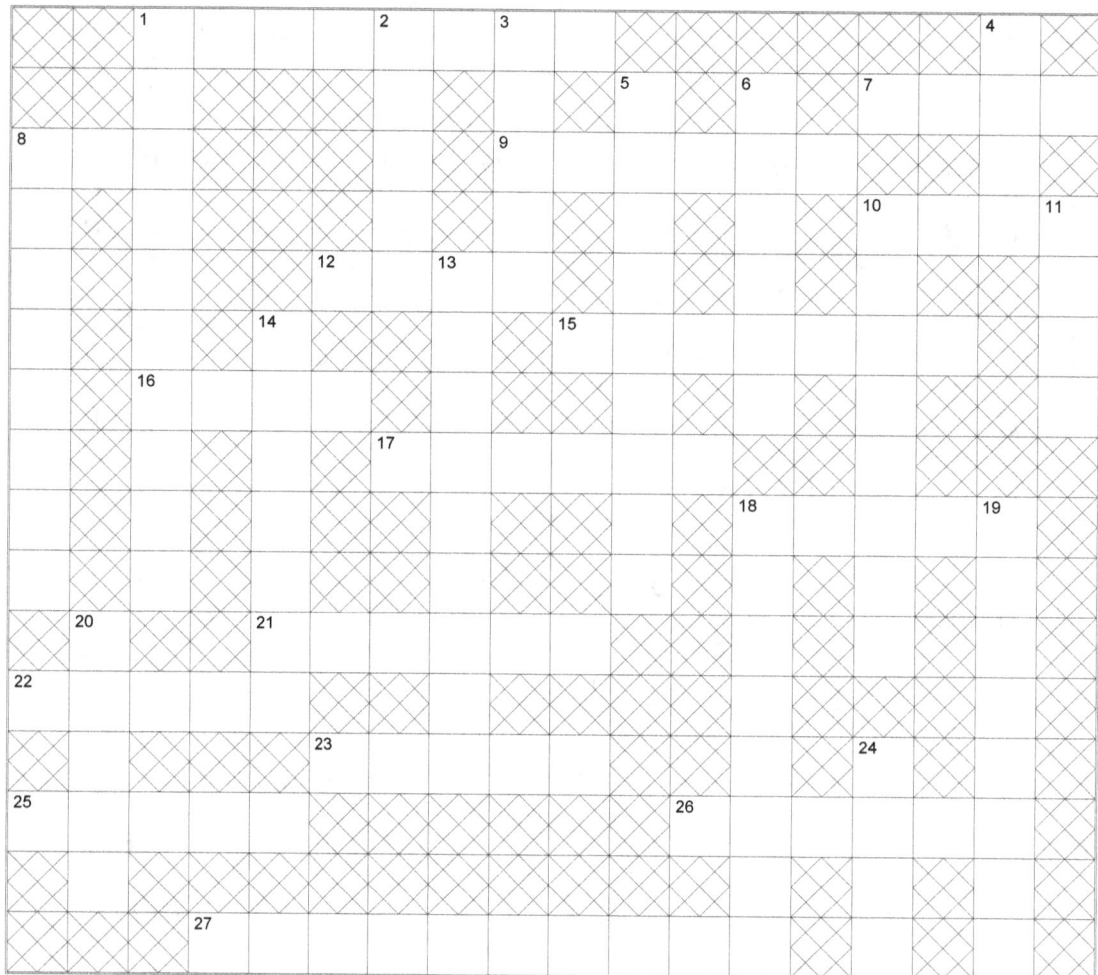

Across
1. Neptune, God of the Sea
7. Killed by Odin
8. Tuesday was named for him
9. Glue on his wings melted when he flew too close to the sun
10. God of Thunder
12. Solemn, aloof god
15. Helped Theseus escape from Labyrinth
16. Ruler of Niflheim
17. Elder Gods
18. Wife of Menelaus, kidnapped by Paris
21. Loved by Persephone and Aphrodite
22. First hero in Europe who undertook a great journey
23. Artemis, the Chief Huntsman
25. Wished for golden touch
26. Golden ____ was the object of Jason's quest
27. Son of Odysseus

Down
1. Lived on Earth and in Underworld
2. First written record of Greece
3. Hunter placed in sky as a constellation
4. Founded Carthage
5. Prison for Minotaur
6. His brother killed Sigurd
8. Account of the creation of the universe and the gods
10. Couldn't reach food or drink
11. Mother of Zeus
13. Sacrificed by Agamemnon for strong winds
14. ____Fields; place of blessedness where good was rewarded
18. Performed twelve labors as a penance
19. Norse Underworld
20. Kidnapped Helen
24. Jupiter, Cheif God

Mythology Crossword 1 Answer Key

		1 P	O	S	2 E	I	3 D	O	N				4 D	
		E			L		R		5 L	6 G	7 Y	M	I	R
8 T	Y	R			I		9 I	C	A	R	U	S		D
H		S			A		O		B		N	10 T	H	O	11 R
E		E		12 O	D	13 I	N		Y		N	A			H
O		P		14 E		P		15 A	R	I	A	D	N	E	E
G		16 H	E	L	A			I			R	T			A
O		O		Y		17 T	I	T	A	N	S	A			
N		N		S				T			18 H	E	L	19 E	N
Y		E		I				H			E	L	U	N	
	20 P		21 A	D	O	N	I	S			R	S	F	
22 J	A	S	O	N			I				C		L	
	R			23 D	I	A	N	A			U	24 Z	H	
25 M	I	D	A	S					26 F	L	E	E	C	E
	S								E			U	I	
		27 T	E	L	E	M	A	C	H	U	S	S	M	

Across
1. Neptune, God of the Sea
7. Killed by Odin
8. Tuesday was named for him
9. Glue on his wings melted when he flew too close to the sun
10. God of Thunder
12. Solemn, aloof god
15. Helped Theseus escape from Labyrinth
16. Ruler of Niflheim
17. Elder Gods
18. Wife of Menelaus, kidnapped by Paris
21. Loved by Persephone and Aphrodite
22. First hero in Europe who undertook a great journey
23. Artemis, the Chief Huntsman
25. Wished for golden touch
26. Golden ____ was the object of Jason's quest
27. Son of Odysseus

Down
1. Lived on Earth and in Underworld
2. First written record of Greece
3. Hunter placed in sky as a constellation
4. Founded Carthage
5. Prison for Minotaur
6. His brother killed Sigurd
8. Account of the creation of the universe and the gods
10. Couldn't reach food or drink
11. Mother of Zeus
13. Sacrificed by Agamemnon for strong winds
14. ____Fields; place of blessedness where good was rewarded
18. Performed twelve labors as a penance
19. Norse Underworld
20. Kidnapped Helen
24. Jupiter, Cheif God

Mythology Crossword 2

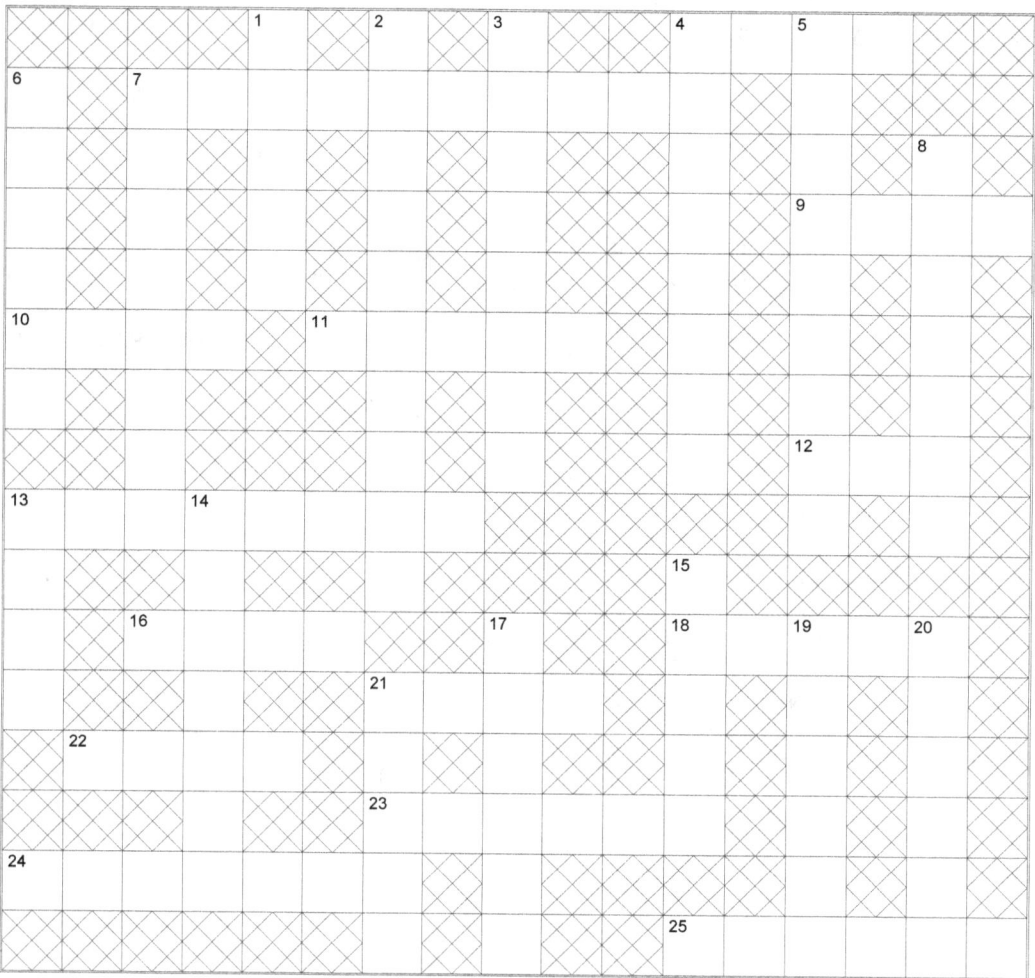

Across
4. Ruler of Niflheim
7. Lived on Earth and in Underworld
9. Killed by Odin
10. Solemn, aloof god
11. First hero in Europe who undertook a great journey
12. Tuesday was named for him
13. Couldn't reach food or drink
16. Jupiter, Cheif God
18. First written record of Greece
21. Founded Carthage
22. Mother of Zeus
23. Founder of the Roman race
24. ____Fields; place of blessedness where good was rewarded
25. Vesta, Goddess of the Hearth

Down
1. Hunter placed in sky as a constellation
2. Son of Odysseus
3. Account of the creation of the universe and the gods
4. Performed twelve labors as a penance
5. Prison for Minotaur
6. Centaur who trained sons of heroes
7. Neptune, God of the Sea
8. Battlefield for men after death
13. God of Thunder
14. Made Athens a commonwealth
15. Wished for golden touch
17. Loved by Persephone and Aphrodite
19. Glue on his wings melted when he flew too close to the sun
20. Location of Apollo's oracle
21. Artemis, the Chief Huntsman

Mythology Crossword 2 Answer Key

			1 O		2 T		3 T		4 H	5 E	L	A	
6 C		7 P	E	R	S	E	P	H	O	N	E		A	
H		O	I		L		E		R			B		8 M
I		S	O		E		O		C			9 Y	M	I	R
R		E	N		M		G		U			R		D
10 O	D	I	N		11 J	A	S	O	N		L		I		G
N		D			C		N		L		E		N		A
		O			H		Y				S		12 T	Y	R
13 T	A	14 N	T	A	L	U	S						H		D
H		H			S						15 M			
O		16 Z	E	U	S		17 A		18 I	L	I	19 A	20 D
R		S			21 D	I	D	O		D		C		E
	22 R	H	E	A		I		O		A		A		L
		U			23 A	E	N	E	A	S		R		P
24 E	L	Y	S	I	A	N		I				U		H
						A		S		25 H	E	S	T	I	A

Across
4. Ruler of Niflheim
7. Lived on Earth and in Underworld
9. Killed by Odin
10. Solemn, aloof god
11. First hero in Europe who undertook a great journey
12. Tuesday was named for him
13. Couldn't reach food or drink
16. Jupiter, Cheif God
18. First written record of Greece
21. Founded Carthage
22. Mother of Zeus
23. Founder of the Roman race
24. ____Fields; place of blessedness where good was rewarded
25. Vesta, Goddess of the Hearth

Down
1. Hunter placed in sky as a constellation
2. Son of Odysseus
3. Account of the creation of the universe and the gods
4. Performed twelve labors as a penance
5. Prison for Minotaur
6. Centaur who trained sons of heroes
7. Neptune, God of the Sea
8. Battlefield for men after death
13. God of Thunder
14. Made Athens a commonwealth
15. Wished for golden touch
17. Loved by Persephone and Aphrodite
19. Glue on his wings melted when he flew too close to the sun
20. Location of Apollo's oracle
21. Artemis, the Chief Huntsman

Mythology Crossword 3

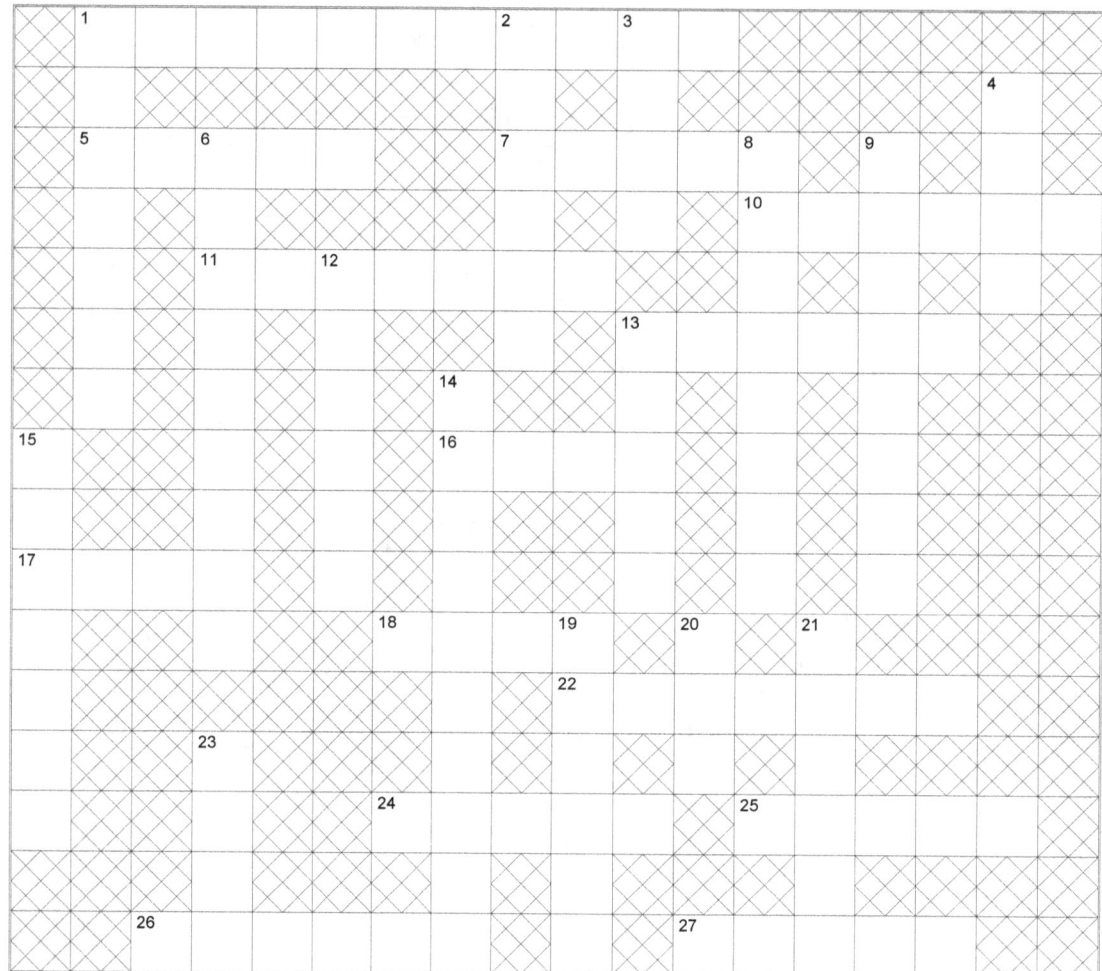

Across
1. Rode Pegasus to kill Chimaera
5. Immeasurable abyss at the beginning of everything
7. Hunter placed in sky as a constellation
10. Glue on his wings melted when he flew too close to the sun
11. Weaver turned into a spider
13. Location of Apollo's oracle
16. Mother of Zeus
17. Founded Carthage
18. Ruler of Niflheim
22. ____Fields; place of blessedness where good was rewarded
24. Wife of Menelaus, kidnapped by Paris
25. Kidnapped Helen
26. Titan father of Zeus
27. First hero in Europe who undertook a great journey

Down
1. Another name for Dionysus
2. Changed into a nightingale
3. Solemn, aloof god
4. Jupiter, Cheif God
6. Sacrificed his daughter
8. Norse Underworld
9. Hall of the Slain
12. Loved by Persephone and Aphrodite
13. Artemis, the Chief Huntsman
14. Gave man the gift of fire
15. Battlefield for men after death
19. Founder of the Roman race
20. Tuesday was named for him
21. Elder Gods
23. God of Thunder

Mythology Crossword 3 Answer Key

		1 B	E	L	L	E	R	O	2 P	H	3 O	N			
		A							R		D				4 Z
	5 C	H	6 A	O	S		7 O	R	I	8 O	N	9 V		E
	C		G				C		N	10 I	C	A	R	U	S
	H		11 A	R	12 A	C	H	N	E		F		L		S
	U		M		D		E		13 D	E	L	P	H	I	
	S		E		O		14 P		I		H		A		
15 M			M		N		16 R	H	E	A			L		
I			N		I		O		N		I		L		
17 D	I	D	O		S		M		A		M		A		
G			N			18 H	E	L	19 A		20 T		21 T		
A							T		22 E	L	Y	S	I	A	N
R			23 T				H		N		R		T		
D			H			24 H	E	L	E	N		25 P	A	R	I	S
			O				U		A				N		
		26 C	R	O	N	U	S		S			27 J	A	S	O	N

Across
1. Rode Pegasus to kill Chimaera
5. Immeasurable abyss at the beginning of everything
7. Hunter placed in sky as a constellation
10. Glue on his wings melted when he flew too close to the sun
11. Weaver turned into a spider
13. Location of Apollo's oracle
16. Mother of Zeus
17. Founded Carthage
18. Ruler of Niflheim
22. ____Fields; place of blessedness where good was rewarded
24. Wife of Menelaus, kidnapped by Paris
25. Kidnapped Helen
26. Titan father of Zeus
27. First hero in Europe who undertook a great journey

Down
1. Another name for Dionysus
2. Changed into a nightingale
3. Solemn, aloof god
4. Jupiter, Cheif God
6. Sacrificed his daughter
8. Norse Underworld
9. Hall of the Slain
12. Loved by Persephone and Aphrodite
13. Artemis, the Chief Huntsman
14. Gave man the gift of fire
15. Battlefield for men after death
19. Founder of the Roman race
20. Tuesday was named for him
21. Elder Gods
23. God of Thunder

Mythology Crossword 4

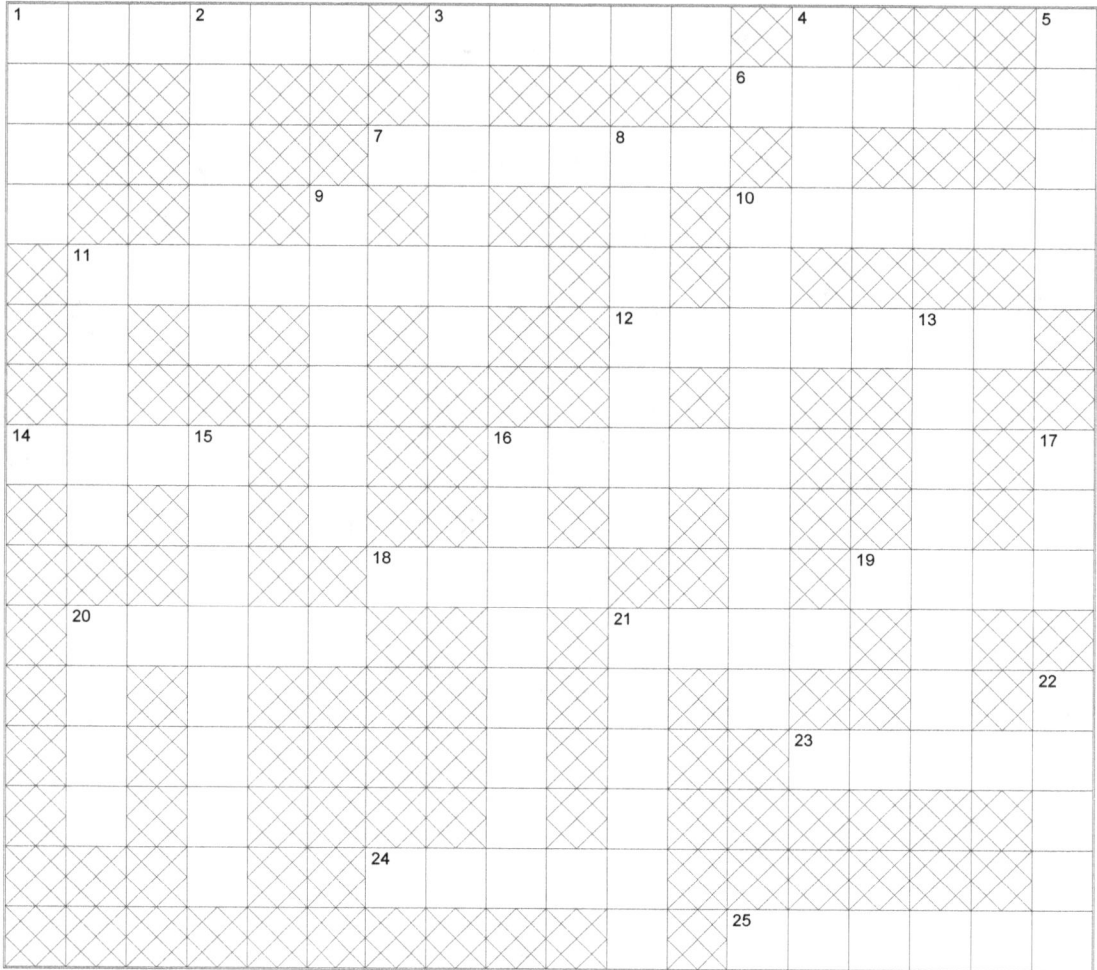

Across
1. Location of Apollo's oracle
3. Immeasurable abyss at the beginning of everything
6. Ruler of Niflheim
7. ____horse; Greeks hid in it to enter Troy
10. Married Cupid
11. Husband of Helen
12. Killed his sister's husband and children
14. Wife of Zeus, Protector of Marriage
16. Artemis, the Chief Huntsman
18. Mother of Zeus
19. God of Thunder
20. Hunter placed in sky as a constellation
21. Besieged city
23. Author of the Iliad and Odyssey
24. First hero in Europe who undertook a great journey
25. Vesta, Goddess of the Hearth

Down
1. Founded Carthage
2. Changed into a nightingale
3. Titan father of Zeus
4. Jupiter, Cheif God
5. Wife of Menelaus, kidnapped by Paris
8. ____Fields; place of blessedness where good was rewarded
9. Golden ____ was the object of Jason's quest
10. Fell in love with a statue
11. Helped Jason
13. Norse Underworld
15. Had a vulnerable heel
16. Creator of Labyrinth
17. Tuesday was named for him
20. Solemn, aloof god
21. Elder Gods
22. Norse goddess of Love and Beauty

Mythology Crossword 4 Answer Key

	1 D	2 E	L	P	H	I		3 C	H	A	O	S		4 Z			5 H
	I		R					R					6 H	E	L	A	E
	D		O			7 W	O	O	D	E	N		U				L
	O		C		9 F		N			L		10 P	S	Y	C	H	E
		11 M	E	N	E	L	A	U	S		Y		Y				N
		E			E		S			12 S	I	G	M	U	13 N	D	
		D			E					I			M		I		
	14 H	E	15 R	A		16 D	I	A	N	A					F		17 T
		A		C		E		A		N			L			L		Y
				H		18 R	H	E	A			19 T	H	O	R	
	20 O	R	I	O	N			D		21 T	R	O	Y		E		
	D			L				A		I			N			I	22 F
	I			L				L		T			23 H	O	M	E	R
	N			E				U		A							E
				S		24 J	A	S	O	N							Y
										25 S	H	E	S	T	I	A

Across
1. Location of Apollo's oracle
3. Immeasurable abyss at the beginning of everything
6. Ruler of Niflheim
7. ____horse; Greeks hid in it to enter Troy
10. Married Cupid
11. Husband of Helen
12. Killed his sister's husband and children
14. Wife of Zeus, Protector of Marriage
16. Artemis, the Chief Huntsman
18. Mother of Zeus
19. God of Thunder
20. Hunter placed in sky as a constellation
21. Besieged city
23. Author of the Iliad and Odyssey
24. First hero in Europe who undertook a great journey
25. Vesta, Goddess of the Hearth

Down
1. Founded Carthage
2. Changed into a nightingale
3. Titan father of Zeus
4. Jupiter, Cheif God
5. Wife of Menelaus, kidnapped by Paris
8. ____Fields; place of blessedness where good was rewarded
9. Golden ____ was the object of Jason's quest
10. Fell in love with a statue
11. Helped Jason
13. Norse Underworld
15. Had a vulnerable heel
16. Creator of Labyrinth
17. Tuesday was named for him
20. Solemn, aloof god
21. Elder Gods
22. Norse goddess of Love and Beauty

Mythology

PHILOMELA	TANTALUS	OEDIPUS	DIANA	PARIS
THESEUS	ELYSIAN	PROCNE	PROMETHEUS	MENELAUS
PENELOPE	PEGASUS	FREE SPACE	MIDGARD	BELLEROPHON
SIGMUND	DAEDALUS	FLEECE	CALLISTO	CHAOS
BRYNHILD	CHIRON	PSYCHE	RHEA	ICARUS

Mythology

DIDO	THOR	TROY	ADONIS	HERCULES
LABYRINTH	HERA	HEPHAESTUS	AENEAS	MINOTAUR
DIONYSUS	AGAMEMNON	FREE SPACE	ILIAD	YMIR
ORION	TYR	GUNNAR	POLYNEICES	CYCLOPS
ARIADNE	TELEMACHUS	BACCHUS	THEOGONY	IPHIGENIA

Mythology

HERCULES	CALLISTO	DIANA	ELYSIAN	FLEECE
SISYPHUS	AMAZONS	RHEA	HERA	BELLEROPHON
MEDEA	AENEAS	FREE SPACE	ASGARD	POLYNEICES
CHAOS	SIGMUND	ATHENA	ODYSSEUS	TANTALUS
TROY	HOMER	ORION	JASON	GUNNAR

Mythology

ODIN	ARIADNE	ARACHNE	PROCNE	LABYRINTH
AGAMEMNON	OEDIPUS	POSEIDON	PYGMALION	THOR
VALHALLA	YMIR	FREE SPACE	NARCISSUS	PLEIADES
DIDO	CRONUS	DIONYSUS	MINOTAUR	MIDAS
ADONIS	THESEUS	PENELOPE	PEGASUS	DELPHI

Mythology

HERCULES	FRIGGA	PHILOMELA	HEPHAESTUS	ELYSIAN
ARIADNE	PROCNE	POSEIDON	THOR	THESEUS
WOODEN	ODYSSEUS	FREE SPACE	PEGASUS	DIONYSUS
FREYA	ASGARD	NARCISSUS	DIANA	NIFLHEIM
FLEECE	PYGMALION	BELLEROPHON	AENEAS	DIDO

Mythology

ZEUS	JASON	PROMETHEUS	YMIR	HERMES
MINOTAUR	BACCHUS	HELA	PERSEPHONE	MENELAUS
HESTIA	HERA	FREE SPACE	CALLISTO	TROY
CRONUS	AGAMEMNON	ATHENA	ARACHNE	ILIAD
SIGMUND	GUNDRUN	THEOGONY	MIDGARD	TITANS

Mythology

TITANS	SIGMUND	PYGMALION	NIFLHEIM	PHILOMELA
HOMER	CHIRON	HERCULES	ARACHNE	THEOGONY
POSEIDON	AGAMEMNON	FREE SPACE	ATALANTA	HEPHAESTUS
RHEA	HERA	HELEN	BACCHUS	THOR
GUNNAR	BRYNHILD	PROCNE	ARIADNE	PSYCHE

Mythology

ADONIS	ODYSSEUS	ODIN	TANTALUS	HERMES
AMAZONS	ELYSIAN	MIDAS	POLYNEICES	NARCISSUS
MINOTAUR	ICARUS	FREE SPACE	ASGARD	CALLISTO
WOODEN	OEDIPUS	HECTOR	ILIAD	ZEUS
HESTIA	CERBERUS	FREYA	SISYPHUS	DIONYSUS

Mythology

PERSEPHONE	CYCLOPS	PROCNE	DIONYSUS	FLEECE
TITANS	ADONIS	ARACHNE	FREYA	HESTIA
ATALANTA	DELPHI	FREE SPACE	PROMETHEUS	CERBERUS
PARIS	IPHIGENIA	TYR	ARIADNE	AGAMEMNON
ICARUS	NARCISSUS	PEGASUS	HECTOR	ILIAD

Mythology

DAEDALUS	TROY	OEDIPUS	DEMETER	POSEIDON
CALLISTO	PLEIADES	ZEUS	MENELAUS	YMIR
TELEMACHUS	CHAOS	FREE SPACE	ACHILLES	RHEA
ANTIGONE	DIDO	HOMER	HELA	AMAZONS
POLYNEICES	WOODEN	MIDAS	MEDEA	ATHENA

Mythology

CYCLOPS	DELPHI	BRYNHILD	ICARUS	POLYNEICES
PEGASUS	MIDGARD	ARIADNE	YMIR	TROY
VALHALLA	ORION	FREE SPACE	CHAOS	TANTALUS
CRONUS	SISYPHUS	ATALANTA	HERMES	DEMETER
PLEIADES	GUNDRUN	DIANA	ASGARD	FRIGGA

Mythology

MENELAUS	HESTIA	ADONIS	IPHIGENIA	CHIRON
TELEMACHUS	HERA	DIDO	PROMETHEUS	ATHENA
ODIN	HEPHAESTUS	FREE SPACE	TYR	FREYA
ZEUS	RHEA	HECTOR	GUNNAR	PSYCHE
MIDAS	ODYSSEUS	CALLISTO	JASON	NARCISSUS

Mythology

HERCULES	MENELAUS	CRONUS	TITANS	ORION
LABYRINTH	WOODEN	NARCISSUS	CHIRON	TYR
BELLEROPHON	HESTIA	FREE SPACE	PARIS	BRYNHILD
HELA	ELYSIAN	ARACHNE	PANDORA	HEPHAESTUS
PROMETHEUS	THOR	TANTALUS	MIDGARD	NIFLHEIM

Mythology

HECTOR	PERSEPHONE	SIGMUND	ANTIGONE	THEOGONY
OEDIPUS	CERBERUS	DIDO	IPHIGENIA	FRIGGA
ARIADNE	TELEMACHUS	FREE SPACE	DEMETER	PENELOPE
ILIAD	CHAOS	FREYA	MINOTAUR	ATALANTA
AMAZONS	PSYCHE	PLEIADES	JASON	BACCHUS

Mythology

ODIN	DIDO	JASON	GUNNAR	SISYPHUS
ODYSSEUS	ADONIS	SIGMUND	ORION	ICARUS
HERCULES	NIFLHEIM	FREE SPACE	FLEECE	THEOGONY
PARIS	DAEDALUS	ELYSIAN	FREYA	ASGARD
MINOTAUR	PROMETHEUS	PANDORA	WOODEN	BACCHUS

Mythology

ATHENA	BELLEROPHON	POLYNEICES	OEDIPUS	ARACHNE
HERA	HOMER	VALHALLA	YMIR	HELA
FRIGGA	HESTIA	FREE SPACE	ANTIGONE	MIDGARD
DIANA	TELEMACHUS	PHILOMELA	PERSEPHONE	CALLISTO
MIDAS	PSYCHE	LABYRINTH	MENELAUS	AGAMEMNON

Mythology

HEPHAESTUS	PARIS	GUNDRUN	AMAZONS	TELEMACHUS
CYCLOPS	AGAMEMNON	ODYSSEUS	PERSEPHONE	CERBERUS
ODIN	YMIR	FREE SPACE	THOR	CHAOS
ARIADNE	DIDO	MINOTAUR	NIFLHEIM	FLEECE
FREYA	TROY	IPHIGENIA	HELA	FRIGGA

Mythology

LABYRINTH	ANTIGONE	DAEDALUS	HESTIA	HERA
HERMES	THESEUS	ADONIS	NARCISSUS	DELPHI
OEDIPUS	ACHILLES	FREE SPACE	PEGASUS	ICARUS
CRONUS	HECTOR	CALLISTO	MIDGARD	ASGARD
PROMETHEUS	ELYSIAN	MENELAUS	TITANS	BELLEROPHON

Mythology

MINOTAUR	YMIR	PHILOMELA	OEDIPUS	TROY
PERSEPHONE	CHAOS	HELA	POLYNEICES	ICARUS
PROCNE	PENELOPE	FREE SPACE	FREYA	CALLISTO
WOODEN	NARCISSUS	BRYNHILD	ORION	AGAMEMNON
MIDGARD	HELEN	TANTALUS	DIANA	DAEDALUS

Mythology

ELYSIAN	AENEAS	BELLEROPHON	AMAZONS	FRIGGA
ATHENA	PSYCHE	ATALANTA	PYGMALION	ILIAD
GUNNAR	HECTOR	FREE SPACE	SIGMUND	MENELAUS
ASGARD	MIDAS	TELEMACHUS	FLEECE	PANDORA
ARIADNE	HOMER	THOR	THEOGONY	ACHILLES

Mythology

GUNDRUN	ORION	ANTIGONE	FRIGGA	DAEDALUS
POSEIDON	LABYRINTH	DIDO	ODIN	TITANS
CRONUS	HELA	FREE SPACE	PHILOMELA	SISYPHUS
GUNNAR	AMAZONS	PROCNE	PERSEPHONE	BELLEROPHON
WOODEN	PLEIADES	HERCULES	ZEUS	MIDAS

Mythology

HEPHAESTUS	TROY	ARIADNE	HERMES	ARACHNE
AENEAS	DIANA	HOMER	PROMETHEUS	HESTIA
NIFLHEIM	MIDGARD	FREE SPACE	MEDEA	IPHIGENIA
AGAMEMNON	DIONYSUS	PEGASUS	POLYNEICES	PYGMALION
NARCISSUS	TELEMACHUS	TANTALUS	CHAOS	TYR

Mythology

HESTIA	NARCISSUS	DEMETER	TROY	ARACHNE
ADONIS	PEGASUS	CRONUS	ACHILLES	THOR
MINOTAUR	DAEDALUS	FREE SPACE	BELLEROPHON	PYGMALION
ELYSIAN	HECTOR	TITANS	PROCNE	HOMER
ARIADNE	DIANA	PSYCHE	GUNNAR	AMAZONS

Mythology

ANTIGONE	PLEIADES	DIDO	CALLISTO	CYCLOPS
TANTALUS	HERA	POSEIDON	PENELOPE	PROMETHEUS
BACCHUS	POLYNEICES	FREE SPACE	CHIRON	PERSEPHONE
VALHALLA	NIFLHEIM	ICARUS	MENELAUS	FRIGGA
ODIN	HEPHAESTUS	PARIS	JASON	ZEUS

Mythology

ICARUS	CERBERUS	HELA	PROCNE	GUNDRUN
HEPHAESTUS	DAEDALUS	OEDIPUS	MEDEA	THESEUS
ATHENA	TROY	FREE SPACE	CYCLOPS	ACHILLES
PROMETHEUS	DIANA	DIDO	THEOGONY	PHILOMELA
FLEECE	ASGARD	BACCHUS	ZEUS	IPHIGENIA

Mythology

AGAMEMNON	DIONYSUS	ORION	HESTIA	MIDGARD
TANTALUS	HELEN	PARIS	AMAZONS	WOODEN
PYGMALION	LABYRINTH	FREE SPACE	PLEIADES	CALLISTO
TITANS	PENELOPE	PANDORA	JASON	BRYNHILD
FRIGGA	HERA	TELEMACHUS	PSYCHE	MINOTAUR

Mythology

MENELAUS	THESEUS	PLEIADES	DEMETER	ODIN
MEDEA	HEPHAESTUS	NIFLHEIM	TYR	ACHILLES
MIDAS	TANTALUS	FREE SPACE	PENELOPE	PERSEPHONE
SISYPHUS	CYCLOPS	TITANS	DIDO	VALHALLA
ATALANTA	FREYA	HERCULES	AMAZONS	GUNNAR

Mythology

CHAOS	ARACHNE	PANDORA	ATHENA	HESTIA
HERMES	ANTIGONE	AGAMEMNON	HECTOR	PROMETHEUS
GUNDRUN	TELEMACHUS	FREE SPACE	JASON	ADONIS
OEDIPUS	HELA	ILIAD	THEOGONY	PHILOMELA
CALLISTO	LABYRINTH	ODYSSEUS	ELYSIAN	PROCNE

Mythology

TELEMACHUS	TYR	TITANS	CHAOS	GUNNAR
HEPHAESTUS	DELPHI	ODYSSEUS	DIONYSUS	THESEUS
AGAMEMNON	SISYPHUS	FREE SPACE	MIDGARD	DEMETER
BELLEROPHON	RHEA	FLEECE	PENELOPE	MENELAUS
ASGARD	CRONUS	MINOTAUR	VALHALLA	BRYNHILD

Mythology

AMAZONS	AENEAS	GUNDRUN	SIGMUND	HERCULES
THEOGONY	MEDEA	FRIGGA	POLYNEICES	CHIRON
HECTOR	ANTIGONE	FREE SPACE	PERSEPHONE	ATHENA
WOODEN	DIANA	PEGASUS	BACCHUS	HOMER
ORION	DAEDALUS	PHILOMELA	HELEN	ELYSIAN

Mythology

BACCHUS	CRONUS	MINOTAUR	TANTALUS	OEDIPUS
THESEUS	HERA	HEPHAESTUS	CERBERUS	LABYRINTH
ODIN	GUNNAR	FREE SPACE	TELEMACHUS	NIFLHEIM
GUNDRUN	ODYSSEUS	AENEAS	BELLEROPHON	ARACHNE
TYR	DEMETER	AMAZONS	FLEECE	DIDO

Mythology

DELPHI	DAEDALUS	ANTIGONE	POLYNEICES	ARIADNE
POSEIDON	PSYCHE	RHEA	PARIS	FRIGGA
HOMER	HELEN	FREE SPACE	ZEUS	ACHILLES
MENELAUS	SISYPHUS	SIGMUND	TITANS	HERCULES
VALHALLA	HECTOR	ICARUS	CALLISTO	ASGARD

Mythology Vocabulary Word List

No.	Word	Clue/Definition
1.	ABASHED	Embarrassed
2.	ACQUIESCE	To consent without protest
3.	ACQUITTAL	A freeing or clearing from a charge or accusation
4.	AMBROSIA	The food of the gods, thought to give immortality
5.	APPEASING	Soothing; pacifying
6.	ARBITER	A judge
7.	ASCRIBED	Attributed to
8.	ATONEMENT	Making amends for an injury or wrong
9.	ATROCIOUSLY	Horribly; cruelly
10.	AUDACITY	Daring; boldness
11.	AUSTERE	Severe; having no decoration
12.	BOWER	A shaded, leafy recess or arbor
13.	CADENCES	Balanced, rhythmic beats
14.	CAPRICIOUS	Impulsive; given to whim
15.	CHAGRINED	Embarrassed due to failure or disappointment
16.	CIRCUMVENT	Go around or bypass
17.	CLAMOR	Loud expression of discontent
18.	COLOSSUS	A huge statue
19.	CONSORTING	Associating with
20.	CONTEMPTIBLE	Despicable
21.	DAUNTLESS	Fearless; not intimidated
22.	DEIFIED	Worshiped as a god
23.	DESOLATE	Barren; lifeless
24.	DESTITUTE	Impoverished; lacking means of subsistence
25.	DILIGENT	Marked by careful, persistent effort
26.	DISCERNING	Distinguishing; perceiving as being different
27.	DISDAINFUL	Showing contempt
28.	DIVINATION	The art of foretelling events by the use of the supernatural
29.	DRYAD	A wood nymph
30.	EMINENTLY	Outstanding; distinguished; of high quality
31.	EMULATE	Compete with successfully
32.	ENAMORED	Inspired with love
33.	ENDOWMENTS	Funds donated to a group or individual
34.	ENTICED	Lured; tempted
35.	EXONERATE	Free from blame
36.	EXPIATING	Making amends; atoning
37.	EXULTANT	Joyful; triumphant
38.	FILIAL	Of a son or a daughter
39.	FUTILITY	Frivolous; having no useful result
40.	HAVOC	Devastation; chaos
41.	HOMAGE	Honor or respect that is shown publicly
42.	IMPLACABLE	Not able to be appeased
43.	INADVERTENTLY	Accidentally
44.	INCALCULABLE	Unpredictability; impossible to foresee
45.	INCARNATE	Given human form
46.	INEVITABLE	Impossible to avoid
47.	INEXORABLE	Not able to be persuaded
48.	INFALLIBLY	Not capable of an error
49.	LAGGARD	Straggler
50.	LAMENTATION	A song or poem that expresses grief or mourning
51.	LOATHED	Detested

Mythology Vocabulary Word List Continued

No.	Word	Clue/Definition
52.	LUDICROUS	Absurd; incongruous
53.	MANIFEST	Clear; understandable
54.	MYTHOLOGY	Stories about the origin of a people, their gods, and heroes
55.	NAIAD	Spirit that lives in brooks and springs
56.	NECTAR	Drink of the gods; undiluted juice of a fruit
57.	NYMPH	Female spirit that represents nature
58.	OMNIPOTENT	All-powerful
59.	OMNISCIENT	Knowing everything
60.	ORACLE	Transmitter of prophecies at a shrine
61.	PALTRY	Trivial; lacking in importance
62.	PEDESTRIAN	Ordinary; not imaginative
63.	PERPETUALLY	Lasting for an unlimited time
64.	PESTILENCE	Fatal epidemic disease
65.	PLAUSIBLE	Having some truth, but open to doubt
66.	PLIANT	Easily bent
67.	PORTENT	Sign; forewarning; omen
68.	PRODIGY	Person who has exceptional talents or powers
69.	PROMONTORY	High ridge of land that juts out into the water
70.	PROTOTYPE	An original that serves as a model
71.	PYRE	Pile of things that can be used for burning corpses
72.	RAIMENT	Clothing
73.	REDOUBTABLE	Arousing fear or awe
74.	RENOWN	Fame
75.	REPUTED	Supposed to; considered to
76.	RETINUE	Messengers; government representatives
77.	ROUT	Disorderly retreat following a defeat
78.	SATYRS	Human-like creature with a goat's ears, horns, and legs
79.	SCUDDING	Skimming along swiftly and easily
80.	SOMBER	Gloomy; depressing
81.	SOOTHSAYER	A prophet
82.	SORDID	Morally degraded
83.	SQUALID	Dirty from poverty or lack of care
84.	SUCCORED	Assisted; helped
85.	SUFFRAGE	The right to vote
86.	SUMPTUOUSLY	Lavishly; suggesting great expense
87.	SUPPLIANT	Asking humbly
88.	SUSCEPTIBLE	Easily affected or influenced
89.	SUSTENANCE	The supporting of life or health
90.	TORRENT	Turbulent or overwhelming flow
91.	TRYST	Meeting arranged by lovers
92.	UNFATHOMABLE	Not able to be understood
93.	UNSULLIED	Not stained or tainted
94.	USURPER	One who takes another's place by authority or force
95.	VINDICTIVE	Unforgiving; seeking revenge

Mythology Vocabulary Fill In The Blanks 1

_____ 1. Knowing everything

_____ 2. The supporting of life or health

_____ 3. Joyful; triumphant

_____ 4. Arousing fear or awe

_____ 5. Free from blame

_____ 6. Skimming along swiftly and easily

_____ 7. Trivial; lacking in importance

_____ 8. Daring; boldness

_____ 9. To consent without protest

_____ 10. Disorderly retreat following a defeat

_____ 11. Worshiped as a god

_____ 12. Barren; lifeless

_____ 13. Compete with successfully

_____ 14. Impulsive; given to whim

_____ 15. An original that serves as a model

_____ 16. Stories about the origin of a people, their gods, and heroes

_____ 17. A shaded, leafy recess or arbor

_____ 18. The right to vote

_____ 19. Horribly; cruelly

_____ 20. Sign; forewarning; omen

Mythology Vocabulary Fill In The Blanks 1 Answer Key

OMNISCIENT	1. Knowing everything
SUSTENANCE	2. The supporting of life or health
EXULTANT	3. Joyful; triumphant
REDOUBTABLE	4. Arousing fear or awe
EXONERATE	5. Free from blame
SCUDDING	6. Skimming along swiftly and easily
PALTRY	7. Trivial; lacking in importance
AUDACITY	8. Daring; boldness
ACQUIESCE	9. To consent without protest
ROUT	10. Disorderly retreat following a defeat
DEIFIED	11. Worshiped as a god
DESOLATE	12. Barren; lifeless
EMULATE	13. Compete with successfully
CAPRICIOUS	14. Impulsive; given to whim
PROTOTYPE	15. An original that serves as a model
MYTHOLOGY	16. Stories about the origin of a people, their gods, and heroes
BOWER	17. A shaded, leafy recess or arbor
SUFFRAGE	18. The right to vote
ATROCIOUSLY	19. Horribly; cruelly
PORTENT	20. Sign; forewarning; omen

Mythology Vocabulary Fill In The Blanks 2

_____ 1. Associating with

_____ 2. Soothing; pacifying

_____ 3. Horribly; cruelly

_____ 4. Embarrassed

_____ 5. Devastation; chaos

_____ 6. Given human form

_____ 7. Accidentally

_____ 8. Loud expression of discontent

_____ 9. One who takes another's place by authority or force

_____ 10. A freeing or clearing from a charge or accusation

_____ 11. Not able to be understood

_____ 12. Of a son or a daughter

_____ 13. The right to vote

_____ 14. Female spirit that represents nature

_____ 15. Joyful; triumphant

_____ 16. Messengers; government representatives

_____ 17. Severe; having no decoration

_____ 18. An original that serves as a model

_____ 19. All-powerful

_____ 20. Knowing everything

Mythology Vocabulary Fill In The Blanks 2 Answer Key

CONSORTING	1. Associating with
APPEASING	2. Soothing; pacifying
ATROCIOUSLY	3. Horribly; cruelly
ABASHED	4. Embarrassed
HAVOC	5. Devastation; chaos
INCARNATE	6. Given human form
INADVERTENTLY	7. Accidentally
CLAMOR	8. Loud expression of discontent
USURPER	9. One who takes another's place by authority or force
ACQUITTAL	10. A freeing or clearing from a charge or accusation
UNFATHOMABLE	11. Not able to be understood
FILIAL	12. Of a son or a daughter
SUFFRAGE	13. The right to vote
NYMPH	14. Female spirit that represents nature
EXULTANT	15. Joyful; triumphant
RETINUE	16. Messengers; government representatives
AUSTERE	17. Severe; having no decoration
PROTOTYPE	18. An original that serves as a model
OMNIPOTENT	19. All-powerful
OMNISCIENT	20. Knowing everything

Mythology Vocabulary Fill In The Blanks 3

_____ 1. Worshiped as a god

_____ 2. Morally degraded

_____ 3. Absurd; incongruous

_____ 4. Associating with

_____ 5. High ridge of land that juts out into the water

_____ 6. Transmitter of prophecies at a shrine

_____ 7. Free from blame

_____ 8. Disorderly retreat following a defeat

_____ 9. Trivial; lacking in importance

_____ 10. Balanced, rhythmic beats

_____ 11. Frivolous; having no useful result

_____ 12. Female spirit that represents nature

_____ 13. Devastation; chaos

_____ 14. The food of the gods, thought to give immortality

_____ 15. All-powerful

_____ 16. A song or poem that expresses grief or mourning

_____ 17. Skimming along swiftly and easily

_____ 18. Attributed to

_____ 19. Turbulent or overwhelming flow

_____ 20. The supporting of life or health

Mythology Vocabulary Fill In The Blanks 3 Answer Key

DEIFIED	1. Worshiped as a god
SORDID	2. Morally degraded
LUDICROUS	3. Absurd; incongruous
CONSORTING	4. Associating with
PROMONTORY	5. High ridge of land that juts out into the water
ORACLE	6. Transmitter of prophecies at a shrine
EXONERATE	7. Free from blame
ROUT	8. Disorderly retreat following a defeat
PALTRY	9. Trivial; lacking in importance
CADENCES	10. Balanced, rhythmic beats
FUTILITY	11. Frivolous; having no useful result
NYMPH	12. Female spirit that represents nature
HAVOC	13. Devastation; chaos
AMBROSIA	14. The food of the gods, thought to give immortality
OMNIPOTENT	15. All-powerful
LAMENTATION	16. A song or poem that expresses grief or mourning
SCUDDING	17. Skimming along swiftly and easily
ASCRIBED	18. Attributed to
TORRENT	19. Turbulent or overwhelming flow
SUSTENANCE	20. The supporting of life or health

Mythology Vocabulary Fill In The Blanks 4

_____ 1. Sign; forewarning; omen

_____ 2. Embarrassed due to failure or disappointment

_____ 3. Skimming along swiftly and easily

_____ 4. Ordinary; not imaginative

_____ 5. Free from blame

_____ 6. A huge statue

_____ 7. Given human form

_____ 8. Dirty from poverty or lack of care

_____ 9. Accidentally

_____ 10. Morally degraded

_____ 11. Fatal epidemic disease

_____ 12. Meeting arranged by lovers

_____ 13. Messengers; government representatives

_____ 14. Gloomy; depressing

_____ 15. All-powerful

_____ 16. Drink of the gods; undiluted juice of a fruit

_____ 17. Arousing fear or awe

_____ 18. Despicable

_____ 19. Unpredictability; impossible to foresee

_____ 20. Unforgiving; seeking revenge

Mythology Vocabulary Fill In The Blanks 4 Answer Key

PORTENT	1. Sign; forewarning; omen
CHAGRINED	2. Embarrassed due to failure or disappointment
SCUDDING	3. Skimming along swiftly and easily
PEDESTRIAN	4. Ordinary; not imaginative
EXONERATE	5. Free from blame
COLOSSUS	6. A huge statue
INCARNATE	7. Given human form
SQUALID	8. Dirty from poverty or lack of care
INADVERTENTLY	9. Accidentally
SORDID	10. Morally degraded
PESTILENCE	11. Fatal epidemic disease
TRYST	12. Meeting arranged by lovers
RETINUE	13. Messengers; government representatives
SOMBER	14. Gloomy; depressing
OMNIPOTENT	15. All-powerful
NECTAR	16. Drink of the gods; undiluted juice of a fruit
REDOUBTABLE	17. Arousing fear or awe
CONTEMPTIBLE	18. Despicable
INCALCULABLE	19. Unpredictability; impossible to foresee
VINDICTIVE	20. Unforgiving; seeking revenge

Mythology Vocabulary Matching 1

___ 1. CONSORTING   A. Balanced, rhythmic beats
___ 2. ATONEMENT   B. Making amends for an injury or wrong
___ 3. INEXORABLE   C. Distinguishing; perceiving as being different
___ 4. SUMPTUOUSLY   D. Clear; understandable
___ 5. PROMONTORY   E. A song or poem that expresses grief or mourning
___ 6. PLAUSIBLE   F. Turbulent or overwhelming flow
___ 7. SATYRS   G. Not able to be persuaded
___ 8. DIVINATION   H. Impulsive; given to whim
___ 9. NYMPH   I. Given human form
___10. INCARNATE   J. Female spirit that represents nature
___11. TORRENT   K. High ridge of land that juts out into the water
___12. DAUNTLESS   L. Having some truth, but open to doubt
___13. ROUT   M. A huge statue
___14. VINDICTIVE   N. Fatal epidemic disease
___15. DISCERNING   O. Human-like creature with a goat's ears, horns, and legs
___16. ARBITER   P. Lavishly; suggesting great expense
___17. LAMENTATION   Q. Unforgiving; seeking revenge
___18. PESTILENCE   R. A judge
___19. ACQUIESCE   S. Despicable
___20. COLOSSUS   T. Fearless; not intimidated
___21. CAPRICIOUS   U. Disorderly retreat following a defeat
___22. CONTEMPTIBLE   V. The right to vote
___23. MANIFEST   W. To consent without protest
___24. CADENCES   X. Associating with
___25. SUFFRAGE   Y. The art of foretelling events by the use of the supernatural

Mythology Vocabulary Matching 1 Answer Key

X - 1.	CONSORTING	A. Balanced, rhythmic beats
B - 2.	ATONEMENT	B. Making amends for an injury or wrong
G - 3.	INEXORABLE	C. Distinguishing; perceiving as being different
P - 4.	SUMPTUOUSLY	D. Clear; understandable
K - 5.	PROMONTORY	E. A song or poem that expresses grief or mourning
L - 6.	PLAUSIBLE	F. Turbulent or overwhelming flow
O - 7.	SATYRS	G. Not able to be persuaded
Y - 8.	DIVINATION	H. Impulsive; given to whim
J - 9.	NYMPH	I. Given human form
I - 10.	INCARNATE	J. Female spirit that represents nature
F - 11.	TORRENT	K. High ridge of land that juts out into the water
T - 12.	DAUNTLESS	L. Having some truth, but open to doubt
U - 13.	ROUT	M. A huge statue
Q - 14.	VINDICTIVE	N. Fatal epidemic disease
C - 15.	DISCERNING	O. Human-like creature with a goat's ears, horns, and legs
R - 16.	ARBITER	P. Lavishly; suggesting great expense
E - 17.	LAMENTATION	Q. Unforgiving; seeking revenge
N - 18.	PESTILENCE	R. A judge
W - 19.	ACQUIESCE	S. Despicable
M - 20.	COLOSSUS	T. Fearless; not intimidated
H - 21.	CAPRICIOUS	U. Disorderly retreat following a defeat
S - 22.	CONTEMPTIBLE	V. The right to vote
D - 23.	MANIFEST	W. To consent without protest
A - 24.	CADENCES	X. Associating with
V - 25.	SUFFRAGE	Y. The art of foretelling events by the use of the supernatural

Mythology Vocabulary Matching 2

___ 1. MYTHOLOGY   A. Human-like creature with a goat's ears, horns, and legs
___ 2. FUTILITY   B. Arousing fear or awe
___ 3. ORACLE   C. Embarrassed
___ 4. PORTENT   D. A freeing or clearing from a charge or accusation
___ 5. PALTRY   E. Impoverished; lacking means of subsistence
___ 6. APPEASING   F. Devastation; chaos
___ 7. SOMBER   G. Gloomy; depressing
___ 8. SUPPLIANT   H. Morally degraded
___ 9. REPUTED   I. Fearless; not intimidated
___10. TRYST   J. Meeting arranged by lovers
___11. ATROCIOUSLY   K. Horribly; cruelly
___12. ACQUITTAL   L. Outstanding; distinguished; of high quality
___13. INEXORABLE   M. Impulsive; given to whim
___14. MANIFEST   N. Transmitter of prophecies at a shrine
___15. ABASHED   O. Turbulent or overwhelming flow
___16. DESTITUTE   P. Trivial; lacking in importance
___17. PYRE   Q. Stories about the origin of a people, their gods, and heroes
___18. HAVOC   R. Not able to be persuaded
___19. EMINENTLY   S. Clear; understandable
___20. DAUNTLESS   T. Soothing; pacifying
___21. REDOUBTABLE   U. Supposed to; considered to
___22. TORRENT   V. Sign; forewarning; omen
___23. CAPRICIOUS   W. Frivolous; having no useful result
___24. SATYRS   X. Asking humbly
___25. SORDID   Y. Pile of things that can be used for burning corpses

Mythology Vocabulary Matching 2 Answer Key

Q - 1. MYTHOLOGY		A. Human-like creature with a goat's ears, horns, and legs
W - 2. FUTILITY		B. Arousing fear or awe
N - 3. ORACLE		C. Embarrassed
V - 4. PORTENT		D. A freeing or clearing from a charge or accusation
P - 5. PALTRY		E. Impoverished; lacking means of subsistence
T - 6. APPEASING		F. Devastation; chaos
G - 7. SOMBER		G. Gloomy; depressing
X - 8. SUPPLIANT		H. Morally degraded
U - 9. REPUTED		I. Fearless; not intimidated
J - 10. TRYST		J. Meeting arranged by lovers
K - 11. ATROCIOUSLY		K. Horribly; cruelly
D - 12. ACQUITTAL		L. Outstanding; distinguished; of high quality
R - 13. INEXORABLE		M. Impulsive; given to whim
S - 14. MANIFEST		N. Transmitter of prophecies at a shrine
C - 15. ABASHED		O. Turbulent or overwhelming flow
E - 16. DESTITUTE		P. Trivial; lacking in importance
Y - 17. PYRE		Q. Stories about the origin of a people, their gods, and heroes
F - 18. HAVOC		R. Not able to be persuaded
L - 19. EMINENTLY		S. Clear; understandable
I - 20. DAUNTLESS		T. Soothing; pacifying
B - 21. REDOUBTABLE		U. Supposed to; considered to
O - 22. TORRENT		V. Sign; forewarning; omen
M - 23. CAPRICIOUS		W. Frivolous; having no useful result
A - 24. SATYRS		X. Asking humbly
H - 25. SORDID		Y. Pile of things that can be used for burning corpses

Mythology Vocabulary Matching 3

___ 1. CAPRICIOUS   A. A judge
___ 2. INADVERTENTLY   B. Accidentally
___ 3. CIRCUMVENT   C. The supporting of life or health
___ 4. INCARNATE   D. Given human form
___ 5. SUPPLIANT   E. High ridge of land that juts out into the water
___ 6. SORDID   F. Morally degraded
___ 7. RETINUE   G. Daring; boldness
___ 8. DILIGENT   H. A shaded, leafy recess or arbor
___ 9. FILIAL   I. Lasting for an unlimited time
___10. PERPETUALLY   J. Clear; understandable
___11. SOMBER   K. All-powerful
___12. AUDACITY   L. Asking humbly
___13. DESOLATE   M. Messengers; government representatives
___14. SUFFRAGE   N. Funds donated to a group or individual
___15. MYTHOLOGY   O. Unpredictability; impossible to foresee
___16. INCALCULABLE   P. Female spirit that represents nature
___17. NYMPH   Q. Stories about the origin of a people, their gods, and heroes
___18. BOWER   R. Go around or bypass
___19. OMNIPOTENT   S. The right to vote
___20. SUSTENANCE   T. Of a son or a daughter
___21. MANIFEST   U. Person who has exceptional talents or powers
___22. PRODIGY   V. Barren; lifeless
___23. ENDOWMENTS   W. Impulsive; given to whim
___24. ARBITER   X. Gloomy; depressing
___25. PROMONTORY   Y. Marked by careful, persistent effort

Mythology Vocabulary Matching 3 Answer Key

W - 1. CAPRICIOUS	A.	A judge
B - 2. INADVERTENTLY	B.	Accidentally
R - 3. CIRCUMVENT	C.	The supporting of life or health
D - 4. INCARNATE	D.	Given human form
L - 5. SUPPLIANT	E.	High ridge of land that juts out into the water
F - 6. SORDID	F.	Morally degraded
M - 7. RETINUE	G.	Daring; boldness
Y - 8. DILIGENT	H.	A shaded, leafy recess or arbor
T - 9. FILIAL	I.	Lasting for an unlimited time
I - 10. PERPETUALLY	J.	Clear; understandable
X - 11. SOMBER	K.	All-powerful
G - 12. AUDACITY	L.	Asking humbly
V - 13. DESOLATE	M.	Messengers; government representatives
S - 14. SUFFRAGE	N.	Funds donated to a group or individual
Q - 15. MYTHOLOGY	O.	Unpredictability; impossible to foresee
O - 16. INCALCULABLE	P.	Female spirit that represents nature
P - 17. NYMPH	Q.	Stories about the origin of a people, their gods, and heroes
H - 18. BOWER	R.	Go around or bypass
K - 19. OMNIPOTENT	S.	The right to vote
C - 20. SUSTENANCE	T.	Of a son or a daughter
J - 21. MANIFEST	U.	Person who has exceptional talents or powers
U - 22. PRODIGY	V.	Barren; lifeless
N - 23. ENDOWMENTS	W.	Impulsive; given to whim
A - 24. ARBITER	X.	Gloomy; depressing
E - 25. PROMONTORY	Y.	Marked by careful, persistent effort

Mythology Vocabulary Matching 4

___ 1. DRYAD   A. Fearless; not intimidated
___ 2. LAGGARD   B. Embarrassed
___ 3. AMBROSIA   C. An original that serves as a model
___ 4. CAPRICIOUS   D. Absurd; incongruous
___ 5. PLIANT   E. Impulsive; given to whim
___ 6. DAUNTLESS   F. Sign; forewarning; omen
___ 7. NYMPH   G. Severe; having no decoration
___ 8. LOATHED   H. Straggler
___ 9. REDOUBTABLE   I. Spirit that lives in brooks and springs
___ 10. PORTENT   J. Female spirit that represents nature
___ 11. CIRCUMVENT   K. Ordinary; not imaginative
___ 12. PEDESTRIAN   L. Go around or bypass
___ 13. DISDAINFUL   M. Easily bent
___ 14. DESOLATE   N. The food of the gods, thought to give immortality
___ 15. INCARNATE   O. Barren; lifeless
___ 16. ABASHED   P. A shaded, leafy recess or arbor
___ 17. AUSTERE   Q. Assisted; helped
___ 18. SUCCORED   R. Impoverished; lacking means of subsistence
___ 19. NAIAD   S. Given human form
___ 20. ENTICED   T. Lured; tempted
___ 21. LUDICROUS   U. Arousing fear or awe
___ 22. BOWER   V. A wood nymph
___ 23. DESTITUTE   W. Showing contempt
___ 24. PROTOTYPE   X. Detested
___ 25. SORDID   Y. Morally degraded

Mythology Vocabulary Matching 4 Answer Key

V - 1. DRYAD	A.	Fearless; not intimidated
H - 2. LAGGARD	B.	Embarrassed
N - 3. AMBROSIA	C.	An original that serves as a model
E - 4. CAPRICIOUS	D.	Absurd; incongruous
M - 5. PLIANT	E.	Impulsive; given to whim
A - 6. DAUNTLESS	F.	Sign; forewarning; omen
J - 7. NYMPH	G.	Severe; having no decoration
X - 8. LOATHED	H.	Straggler
U - 9. REDOUBTABLE	I.	Spirit that lives in brooks and springs
F - 10. PORTENT	J.	Female spirit that represents nature
L - 11. CIRCUMVENT	K.	Ordinary; not imaginative
K - 12. PEDESTRIAN	L.	Go around or bypass
W - 13. DISDAINFUL	M.	Easily bent
O - 14. DESOLATE	N.	The food of the gods, thought to give immortality
S - 15. INCARNATE	O.	Barren; lifeless
B - 16. ABASHED	P.	A shaded, leafy recess or arbor
G - 17. AUSTERE	Q.	Assisted; helped
Q - 18. SUCCORED	R.	Impoverished; lacking means of subsistence
I - 19. NAIAD	S.	Given human form
T - 20. ENTICED	T.	Lured; tempted
D - 21. LUDICROUS	U.	Arousing fear or awe
P - 22. BOWER	V.	A wood nymph
R - 23. DESTITUTE	W.	Showing contempt
C - 24. PROTOTYPE	X.	Detested
Y - 25. SORDID	Y.	Morally degraded

Mythology Vocabulary Magic Squares 1

Match the definition with the vocabulary word. Put your answers in the magic squares below. When your answers are correct, all columns and rows will add to the same number.

A. ARBITER
B. OMNIPOTENT
C. UNSULLIED
D. PRODIGY
E. CHAGRINED
F. RAIMENT
G. FUTILITY
H. EMINENTLY
I. RENOWN
J. ORACLE
K. INCARNATE
L. UNFATHOMABLE
M. INEXORABLE
N. BOWER
O. ACQUIESCE
P. AMBROSIA

1. Clothing
2. Fame
3. To consent without protest
4. Person who has exceptional talents or powers
5. Not able to be persuaded
6. All-powerful
7. Outstanding; distinguished; of high quality
8. Given human form
9. Not stained or tainted
10. The food of the gods, thought to give immortality
11. Transmitter of prophecies at a shrine
12. Embarrassed due to failure or disappointment
13. Not able to be understood
14. Frivolous; having no useful result
15. A judge
16. A shaded, leafy recess or arbor

A= 15	B= 6	C= 9	D= 4
E= 12	F= 1	G= 14	H= 7
I= 2	J= 11	K= 8	L= 13
M= 5	N= 16	O= 3	P= 10

Mythology Vocabulary Magic Squares 1 Answer Key

Match the definition with the vocabulary word. Put your answers in the magic squares below. When your answers are correct, all columns and rows will add to the same number.

A. ARBITER
B. OMNIPOTENT
C. UNSULLIED
D. PRODIGY
E. CHAGRINED
F. RAIMENT
G. FUTILITY
H. EMINENTLY
I. RENOWN
J. ORACLE
K. INCARNATE
L. UNFATHOMABLE
M. INEXORABLE
N. BOWER
O. ACQUIESCE
P. AMBROSIA

1. Clothing
2. Fame
3. To consent without protest
4. Person who has exceptional talents or powers
5. Not able to be persuaded
6. All-powerful
7. Outstanding; distinguished; of high quality
8. Given human form
9. Not stained or tainted
10. The food of the gods, thought to give immortality
11. Transmitter of prophecies at a shrine
12. Embarrassed due to failure or disappointment
13. Not able to be understood
14. Frivolous; having no useful result
15. A judge
16. A shaded, leafy recess or arbor

A=15	B=6	C=9	D=4
E=12	F=1	G=14	H=7
I=2	J=11	K=8	L=13
M=5	N=16	O=3	P=10

Mythology Vocabulary Magic Squares 2

Match the definition with the vocabulary word. Put your answers in the magic squares below. When your answers are correct, all columns and rows will add to the same number.

A. LAGGARD
B. CHAGRINED
C. USURPER
D. CADENCES
E. ASCRIBED
F. SATYRS
G. HAVOC
H. ABASHED
I. AUSTERE
J. AUDACITY
K. PESTILENCE
L. LUDICROUS
M. PROTOTYPE
N. DISCERNING
O. ATROCIOUSLY
P. LAMENTATION

1. An original that serves as a model
2. Human-like creature with a goat's ears, horns, and legs
3. Embarrassed
4. Horribly; cruelly
5. Absurd; incongruous
6. One who takes another's place by authority or force
7. Straggler
8. Daring; boldness
9. Fatal epidemic disease
10. Balanced, rhythmic beats
11. Embarrassed due to failure or disappointment
12. Severe; having no decoration
13. Distinguishing; perceiving as being different
14. Attributed to
15. Devastation; chaos
16. A song or poem that expresses grief or mourning

A=	B=	C=	D=
E=	F=	G=	H=
I=	J=	K=	L=
M=	N=	O=	P=

Mythology Vocabulary Magic Squares 2 Answer Key

Match the definition with the vocabulary word. Put your answers in the magic squares below. When your answers are correct, all columns and rows will add to the same number.

A. LAGGARD
B. CHAGRINED
C. USURPER
D. CADENCES
E. ASCRIBED
F. SATYRS
G. HAVOC
H. ABASHED
I. AUSTERE
J. AUDACITY
K. PESTILENCE
L. LUDICROUS
M. PROTOTYPE
N. DISCERNING
O. ATROCIOUSLY
P. LAMENTATION

1. An original that serves as a model
2. Human-like creature with a goat's ears, horns, and legs
3. Embarrassed
4. Horribly; cruelly
5. Absurd; incongruous
6. One who takes another's place by authority or force
7. Straggler
8. Daring; boldness
9. Fatal epidemic disease
10. Balanced, rhythmic beats
11. Embarrassed due to failure or disappointment
12. Severe; having no decoration
13. Distinguishing; perceiving as being different
14. Attributed to
15. Devastation; chaos
16. A song or poem that expresses grief or mourning

A=7	B=11	C=6	D=10
E=14	F=2	G=15	H=3
I=12	J=8	K=9	L=5
M=1	N=13	O=4	P=16

Mythology Vocabulary Magic Squares 3

Match the definition with the vocabulary word. Put your answers in the magic squares below. When your answers are correct, all columns and rows will add to the same number.

A. REDOUBTABLE
B. SATYRS
C. PROTOTYPE
D. MANIFEST
E. LUDICROUS
F. ATROCIOUSLY
G. LAGGARD
H. EMULATE
I. INEXORABLE
J. PERPETUALLY
K. ENAMORED
L. LAMENTATION
M. DIVINATION
N. NYMPH
O. DAUNTLESS
P. CONSORTING

1. An original that serves as a model
2. Lasting for an unlimited time
3. Horribly; cruelly
4. Fearless; not intimidated
5. Associating with
6. Absurd; incongruous
7. Not able to be persuaded
8. Clear; understandable
9. The art of foretelling events by the use of the supernatural
10. Compete with successfully
11. A song or poem that expresses grief or mourning
12. Arousing fear or awe
13. Human-like creature with a goat's ears, horns, and legs
14. Inspired with love
15. Straggler
16. Female spirit that represents nature

A=	B=	C=	D=
E=	F=	G=	H=
I=	J=	K=	L=
M=	N=	O=	P=

Mythology Vocabulary Magic Squares 3 Answer Key

Match the definition with the vocabulary word. Put your answers in the magic squares below. When your answers are correct, all columns and rows will add to the same number.

A. REDOUBTABLE
B. SATYRS
C. PROTOTYPE
D. MANIFEST
E. LUDICROUS
F. ATROCIOUSLY
G. LAGGARD
H. EMULATE
I. INEXORABLE
J. PERPETUALLY
K. ENAMORED
L. LAMENTATION
M. DIVINATION
N. NYMPH
O. DAUNTLESS
P. CONSORTING

1. An original that serves as a model
2. Lasting for an unlimited time
3. Horribly; cruelly
4. Fearless; not intimidated
5. Associating with
6. Absurd; incongruous
7. Not able to be persuaded
8. Clear; understandable
9. The art of foretelling events by the use of the supernatural
10. Compete with successfully
11. A song or poem that expresses grief or mourning
12. Arousing fear or awe
13. Human-like creature with a goat's ears, horns, and legs
14. Inspired with love
15. Straggler
16. Female spirit that represents nature

A=12	B=13	C=1	D=8
E=6	F=3	G=15	H=10
I=7	J=2	K=14	L=11
M=9	N=16	O=4	P=5

Mythology Vocabulary Magic Squares 4

Match the definition with the vocabulary word. Put your answers in the magic squares below. When your answers are correct, all columns and rows will add to the same number.

A. ENAMORED
B. PROTOTYPE
C. USURPER
D. INFALLIBLY
E. DILIGENT
F. PORTENT
G. TRYST
H. ENDOWMENTS
I. EXPIATING
J. AUDACITY
K. PRODIGY
L. LAGGARD
M. REDOUBTABLE
N. SUFFRAGE
O. CADENCES
P. CIRCUMVENT

1. Balanced, rhythmic beats
2. Daring; boldness
3. Funds donated to a group or individual
4. Inspired with love
5. Not capable of an error
6. Marked by careful, persistent effort
7. Person who has exceptional talents or powers
8. The right to vote
9. Sign; forewarning; omen
10. One who takes another's place by authority or force
11. Arousing fear or awe
12. Straggler
13. Making amends; atoning
14. Go around or bypass
15. An original that serves as a model
16. Meeting arranged by lovers

A=	B=	C=	D=
E=	F=	G=	H=
I=	J=	K=	L=
M=	N=	O=	P=

Mythology Vocabulary Magic Squares 4 Answer Key

Match the definition with the vocabulary word. Put your answers in the magic squares below. When your answers are correct, all columns and rows will add to the same number.

A. ENAMORED
B. PROTOTYPE
C. USURPER
D. INFALLIBLY
E. DILIGENT
F. PORTENT
G. TRYST
H. ENDOWMENTS
I. EXPIATING
J. AUDACITY
K. PRODIGY
L. LAGGARD
M. REDOUBTABLE
N. SUFFRAGE
O. CADENCES
P. CIRCUMVENT

1. Balanced, rhythmic beats
2. Daring; boldness
3. Funds donated to a group or individual
4. Inspired with love
5. Not capable of an error
6. Marked by careful, persistent effort
7. Person who has exceptional talents or powers
8. The right to vote
9. Sign; forewarning; omen
10. One who takes another's place by authority or force
11. Arousing fear or awe
12. Straggler
13. Making amends; atoning
14. Go around or bypass
15. An original that serves as a model
16. Meeting arranged by lovers

A=4	B=15	C=10	D=5
E=6	F=9	G=16	H=3
I=13	J=2	K=7	L=12
M=11	N=8	O=1	P=14

Mythology Vocabulary Word Search 1

```
S P L N A I A D E H T A O L H F W Y J
U E A T U P A L T R Y K K P L I A S Q M
F S M H D L J D N T E T B G T L V O P H
F T E T A L U M E T Y P P W O I O O H C
R I N L C R S O M B E R U N R A C T A G
A L T M I E U N I T E R T T R L V H T P
G E A N T P L A U S I B L E I Y S R S
E N T X Y N X L R M N P N T N D R A O W
L C I D G M O O S X C J A E T Y T Y C Z
A E O B R S N Q N Z H N X J T C V E I J
G F N R E Y B O W E R O N A E K Y R O C
G U L D M G A N L A R D S N E B O D U H
A T Y P D I J D C A E T M N U A E S Y
R I H C A D P N B R S N T F T N B I L S
D L U L U O I L O R A C L E I S A F Y L
Z I S A N R E M I I E R U G C U S I Z
X T U M T P A T L A G N B D E L H E Y R
R Y R O L N V P R M M Z O I D L E D K X
L F P R E L P F C Y F T N W T I D K P L
E R E T S U A M T F S E M I N E N T L Y
P Y R E S E C N A N E T S U S D R G V Y
```

A judge (7)
A prophet (10)
A shaded, leafy recess or arbor (5)
A song or poem that expresses grief or mourning (11)
A wood nymph (5)
Asking humbly (9)
Barren; lifeless (8)
Clothing (7)
Compete with successfully (7)
Daring; boldness (8)
Detested (7)
Devastation; chaos (5)
Disorderly retreat following a defeat (4)
Drink of the gods; undiluted juice of a fruit (6)
Easily bent (6)
Embarrassed (7)
Fame (6)
Fatal epidemic disease (10)
Fearless; not intimidated (9)
Female spirit that represents nature (5)
Free from blame (9)
Frivolous; having no useful result (8)
Given human form (9)
Gloomy; depressing (6)
Having some truth, but open to doubt (9)
Horribly; cruelly (11)

Human-like creature with a goat's ears, horns, and legs (6)
Inspired with love (8)
Loud expression of discontent (6)
Lured; tempted (7)
Meeting arranged by lovers (5)
Messengers; government representatives (7)
Not able to be persuaded (10)
Not stained or tainted (9)
Of a son or a daughter (6)
One who takes another's place by authority or force (7)
Outstanding; distinguished; of high quality (9)
Person who has exceptional talents or powers (7)
Pile of things that can be used for burning corpses (4)
Severe; having no decoration (7)
Skimming along swiftly and easily (8)
Spirit that lives in brooks and springs (5)
Straggler (7)
Supposed to; considered to (7)
The right to vote (8)
The supporting of life or health (10)
Transmitter of prophecies at a shrine (6)
Trivial; lacking in importance (6)
Turbulent or overwhelming flow (7)
Worshiped as a god (7)

Mythology Vocabulary Word Search 1 Answer Key

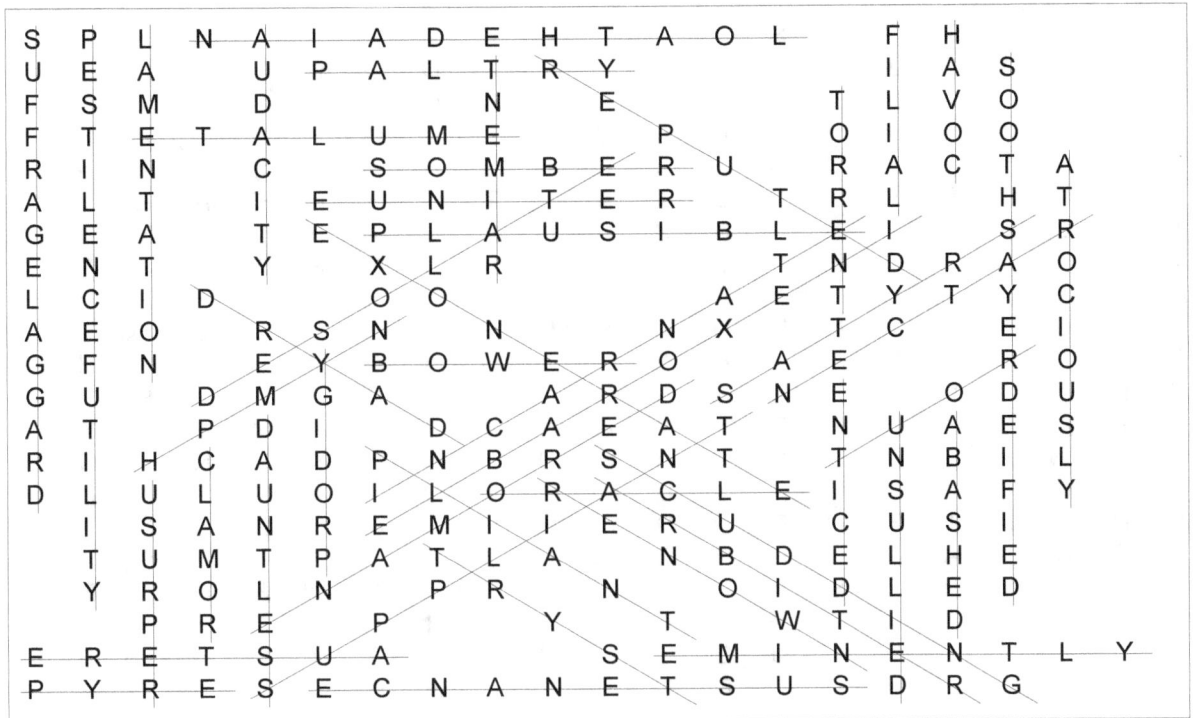

A judge (7)
A prophet (10)
A shaded, leafy recess or arbor (5)
A song or poem that expresses grief or mourning (11)
A wood nymph (5)
Asking humbly (9)
Barren; lifeless (8)
Clothing (7)
Compete with successfully (7)
Daring; boldness (8)
Detested (7)
Devastation; chaos (5)
Disorderly retreat following a defeat (4)
Drink of the gods; undiluted juice of a fruit (6)
Easily bent (6)
Embarrassed (7)
Fame (6)
Fatal epidemic disease (10)
Fearless; not intimidated (9)
Female spirit that represents nature (5)
Free from blame (9)
Frivolous; having no useful result (8)
Given human form (9)
Gloomy; depressing (6)
Having some truth, but open to doubt (9)
Horribly; cruelly (11)

Human-like creature with a goat's ears, horns, and legs (6)
Inspired with love (8)
Loud expression of discontent (6)
Lured; tempted (7)
Meeting arranged by lovers (5)
Messengers; government representatives (7)
Not able to be persuaded (10)
Not stained or tainted (9)
Of a son or a daughter (6)
One who takes another's place by authority or force (7)
Outstanding; distinguished; of high quality (9)
Person who has exceptional talents or powers (7)
Pile of things that can be used for burning corpses (4)
Severe; having no decoration (7)
Skimming along swiftly and easily (8)
Spirit that lives in brooks and springs (5)
Straggler (7)
Supposed to; considered to (7)
The right to vote (8)
The supporting of life or health (10)
Transmitter of prophecies at a shrine (6)
Trivial; lacking in importance (6)
Turbulent or overwhelming flow (7)
Worshiped as a god (7)

Mythology Vocabulary Word Search 2

```
F I L I A L U S U R P E R T P N P D B H
A X M N S J A S C R I B E D Q C Y N O Y
C S T R V Y Q D O S A B N G A D S M Y K
Q A N A I A D I L A U Q S D D U A L P N
U C A I S K C S O K D S E N S G D O T H
I Q I M R F Z D S T A N T C E E G A E Z
T U L E Y X D A S S C H E E T F D T M B
T I P N T R F I U E I P P U N R J H U S
A E X T A V D N S F T L P J A A M E L R
L S G T S P R F P I Y E G G V Z N D A Y
D C C I I E A U B N R N G H A V O C T H
R E T I N U E L B A C A L P M I L T E V
N P I O E C E D T M L M B P Y A R L N X
C J W F V P A Q C R R O H A M Y B K T K
O N G B I K Y R V L Y R O S A T T I L
A R B I T E R R N S D E R T R H N D C J
S O A B A R D E E A W D D O P E E I E P
K U C C B J S B W O T A X B T W R D D B
Z T T V L M T M B B Y E B R T C R R M J
X H X C E E V O G R N M O N G R O O V G
A U S T E R E S D I G P Z N B S T S J L
```

A freeing or clearing from a charge or accusation (9)
A huge statue (8)
A judge (7)
A shaded, leafy recess or arbor (5)
A wood nymph (5)
Attributed to (8)
Balanced, rhythmic beats (8)
Clear; understandable (8)
Clothing (7)
Compete with successfully (7)
Daring; boldness (8)
Detested (7)
Devastation; chaos (5)
Dirty from poverty or lack of care (7)
Disorderly retreat following a defeat (4)
Drink of the gods; undiluted juice of a fruit (6)
Easily affected or influenced (11)
Easily bent (6)
Embarrassed (7)
Fame (6)
Female spirit that represents nature (5)
Given human form (9)
Gloomy; depressing (6)
Honor or respect that is shown publicly (6)
Human-like creature with a goat's ears, horns, and legs (6)

Impossible to avoid (10)
Inspired with love (8)
Loud expression of discontent (6)
Lured; tempted (7)
Meeting arranged by lovers (5)
Messengers; government representatives (7)
Morally degraded (6)
Not able to be appeased (10)
Not able to be persuaded (10)
Of a son or a daughter (6)
One who takes another's place by authority or force (7)
Pile of things that can be used for burning corpses (4)
Severe; having no decoration (7)
Showing contempt (10)
Sign; forewarning; omen (7)
Spirit that lives in brooks and springs (5)
Straggler (7)
Supposed to; considered to (7)
The supporting of life or health (10)
To consent without protest (9)
Transmitter of prophecies at a shrine (6)
Trivial; lacking in importance (6)
Turbulent or overwhelming flow (7)
Worshiped as a god (7)

Mythology Vocabulary Word Search 2 Answer Key

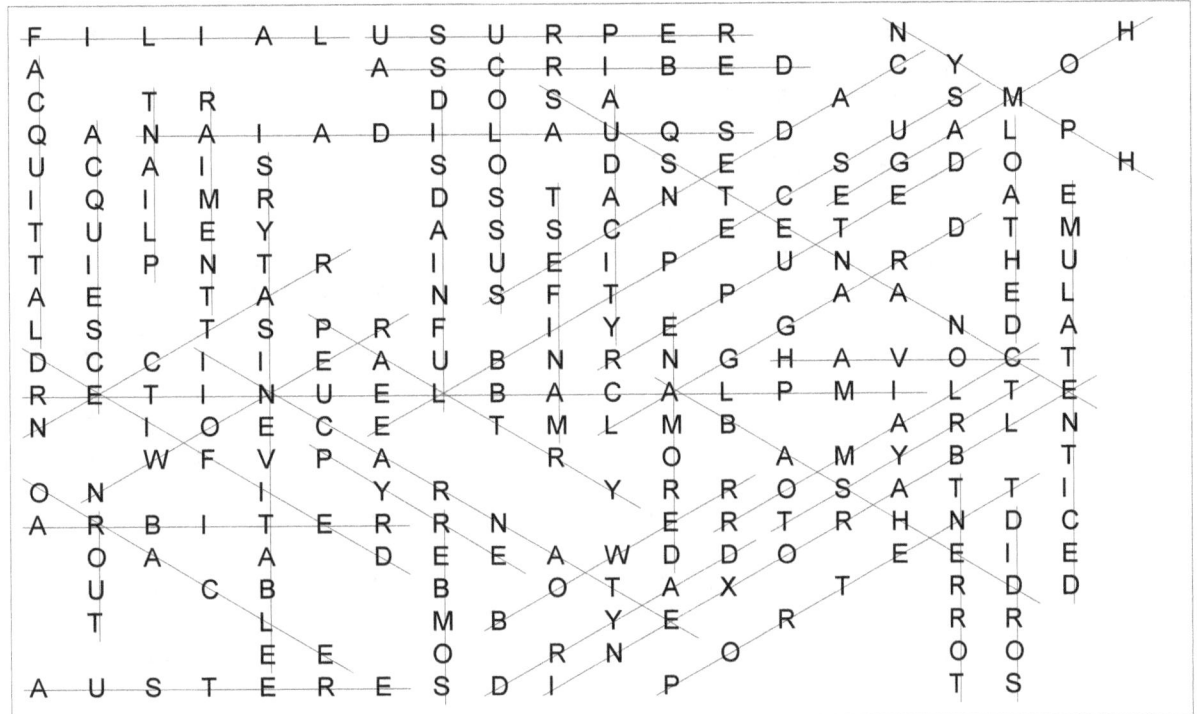

A freeing or clearing from a charge or accusation (9)
A huge statue (8)
A judge (7)
A shaded, leafy recess or arbor (5)
A wood nymph (5)
Attributed to (8)
Balanced, rhythmic beats (8)
Clear; understandable (8)
Clothing (7)
Compete with successfully (7)
Daring; boldness (8)
Detested (7)
Devastation; chaos (5)
Dirty from poverty or lack of care (7)
Disorderly retreat following a defeat (4)
Drink of the gods; undiluted juice of a fruit (6)
Easily affected or influenced (11)
Easily bent (6)
Embarrassed (7)
Fame (6)
Female spirit that represents nature (5)
Given human form (9)
Gloomy; depressing (6)
Honor or respect that is shown publicly (6)
Human-like creature with a goat's ears, horns, and legs (6)

Impossible to avoid (10)
Inspired with love (8)
Loud expression of discontent (6)
Lured; tempted (7)
Meeting arranged by lovers (5)
Messengers; government representatives (7)
Morally degraded (6)
Not able to be appeased (10)
Not able to be persuaded (10)
Of a son or a daughter (6)
One who takes another's place by authority or force (7)
Pile of things that can be used for burning corpses (4)
Severe; having no decoration (7)
Showing contempt (10)
Sign; forewarning; omen (7)
Spirit that lives in brooks and springs (5)
Straggler (7)
Supposed to; considered to (7)
The supporting of life or health (10)
To consent without protest (9)
Transmitter of prophecies at a shrine (6)
Trivial; lacking in importance (6)
Turbulent or overwhelming flow (7)
Worshiped as a god (7)

Mythology Vocabulary Word Search 3

```
U A H P T N E C T A R X G P F I L I A L
N S O R N C E L B I T P M E T N O C J L
S C M O E X F N K S C U D D I N G R P A
U R A M M T S A P D F V M E X G M P H M
L I G O I W M S M M E J C S S X E S Z F
L B E N A B B Y Y C R S Y T N A H N C H
I E S T R Y R T L A P Y T R S S Y L Z J
E D L O A T H E D R Y A D I O R A C L X
D W S R M O T C S R L F N A T M O T S E
K I V Y L B A P Z E T G X N O U T U A N
A S C O V D E C I T N E T R O P T C T W
P H G O E E R R N I E A X T E B O E Y X
Y Y V N L R E L Y N N E I B Z N Y M R H
R R C C B O T Z M U I K X A S V O D S B
E E I A O C S B P E M T R O D O E W T Y
S V R P W C U S H W E S R G N H R I N S
D I C R E U A L U V X T R Y S E C D A L
I T U I R S S A W S I T R A S A R T I X
L C M C H U X G X N N N B E D T T A E R
I I V I H R Y G G E G A L U P I Q T T D
G D E O A P G A R P V I A Q U U I X R R
E N N U V E Q R V J W Q H B T Y F E Q
N I T S O R O D S R Y P C L R N R E B K
T V R H C T S E F I N A M A L R J R D V
```

ABASHED	CIRCUMVENT	FILIAL	PALTRY	SATYRS
ACQUITTAL	CLAMOR	HAVOC	PEDESTRIAN	SCUDDING
AMBROSIA	COLOSSUS	HOMAGE	PLIANT	SOMBER
APPEASING	CONSORTING	LAGGARD	PORTENT	SORDID
ARBITER	CONTEMPTIBLE	LOATHED	PROMONTORY	SUCCORED
ASCRIBED	DESTITUTE	MANIFEST	PYRE	TORRENT
AUDACITY	DILIGENT	MYTHOLOGY	RAIMENT	TRYST
AUSTERE	DRYAD	NAIAD	RENOWN	UNSULLIED
BOWER	EMINENTLY	NECTAR	REPUTED	USURPER
CADENCES	ENTICED	NYMPH	RETINUE	VINDICTIVE
CAPRICIOUS	EXONERATE	ORACLE	ROUT	

Mythology Vocabulary Word Search 3 Answer Key

ABASHED	CIRCUMVENT	FILIAL	PALTRY	SATYRS
ACQUITTAL	CLAMOR	HAVOC	PEDESTRIAN	SCUDDING
AMBROSIA	COLOSSUS	HOMAGE	PLIANT	SOMBER
APPEASING	CONSORTING	LAGGARD	PORTENT	SORDID
ARBITER	CONTEMPTIBLE	LOATHED	PROMONTORY	SUCCORED
ASCRIBED	DESTITUTE	MANIFEST	PYRE	TORRENT
AUDACITY	DILIGENT	MYTHOLOGY	RAIMENT	TRYST
AUSTERE	DRYAD	NAIAD	RENOWN	UNSULLIED
BOWER	EMINENTLY	NECTAR	REPUTED	USURPER
CADENCES	ENTICED	NYMPH	RETINUE	VINDICTIVE
CAPRICIOUS	EXONERATE	ORACLE	ROUT	

Mythology Vocabulary Word Search 4

```
E G A R F F U S T P E R P E T U A L L Y
L S R S N P S N R O Y G P R N B Q B D J
B Q O U D K E J Y L R R H S S O G B R Z
I U U P E G X S S R T R U X C W G C A Y
T A T P I H P X T L E L E L S E H L I A
P L V L F L I R A I L T X N R H U G M F
M I I I I B A P O I L B I E T D P B E L
E D N A E A T P E T N E P N I H R F N V
T X N N D U I D P D O R N C U O O X T Z
N T O T W S N P E E U T R C S E D T X H
O J H N Y T G N X S A O Y I E D I F P N
C K G W E E I Y U U U S A P L J G M C H
Y N D I D R O S A S C R I B E D Y K I Q
P Y H H G E A V K T O M P N B N B K R D
A V Q A O S Z T X E F M V Y G B B B C V
W U H F F M X R E N P I B D R Y A D U L
H C D E H S A B A A T O N E M E N T M P
A L E A R C R G D N L E R C R R B F V D
V O R O C N B E E C L A M T A N M I E P
O A O R L I I V N E J B G U E R A L N J
C T M A A E T A L O S E D G L N N I T V
W H A C M K E Y M Y W L W M A A T A A Y
H E N L O C R A T C E N W V Q R T L T D
B D E E R O M N I S C I E N T Q D E H E
```

ABASHED	CLAMOR	HAVOC	PALTRY	ROUT
AMBROSIA	CONTEMPTIBLE	HOMAGE	PERPETUALLY	SOMBER
APPEASING	DEIFIED	INCARNATE	PESTILENCE	SORDID
ARBITER	DESOLATE	LAGGARD	PLIANT	SQUALID
ASCRIBED	DILIGENT	LOATHED	PORTENT	SUFFRAGE
ATONEMENT	DRYAD	LUDICROUS	PRODIGY	SUPPLIANT
AUDACITY	EMULATE	NAIAD	PROTOTYPE	SUSTENANCE
AUSTERE	ENAMORED	NECTAR	PYRE	TORRENT
BOWER	EXONERATE	NYMPH	RAIMENT	TRYST
CHAGRINED	EXPIATING	OMNISCIENT	RENOWN	UNSULLIED
CIRCUMVENT	FILIAL	ORACLE	RETINUE	USURPER

Mythology Vocabulary Word Search 4 Answer Key

ABASHED	CLAMOR	HAVOC	PALTRY	ROUT
AMBROSIA	CONTEMPTIBLE	HOMAGE	PERPETUALLY	SOMBER
APPEASING	DEIFIED	INCARNATE	PESTILENCE	SORDID
ARBITER	DESOLATE	LAGGARD	PLIANT	SQUALID
ASCRIBED	DILIGENT	LOATHED	PORTENT	SUFFRAGE
ATONEMENT	DRYAD	LUDICROUS	PRODIGY	SUPPLIANT
AUDACITY	EMULATE	NAIAD	PROTOTYPE	SUSTENANCE
AUSTERE	ENAMORED	NECTAR	PYRE	TORRENT
BOWER	EXONERATE	NYMPH	RAIMENT	TRYST
CHAGRINED	EXPIATING	OMNISCIENT	RENOWN	UNSULLIED
CIRCUMVENT	FILIAL	ORACLE	RETINUE	USURPER

Mythology Vocabulary Crossword 1

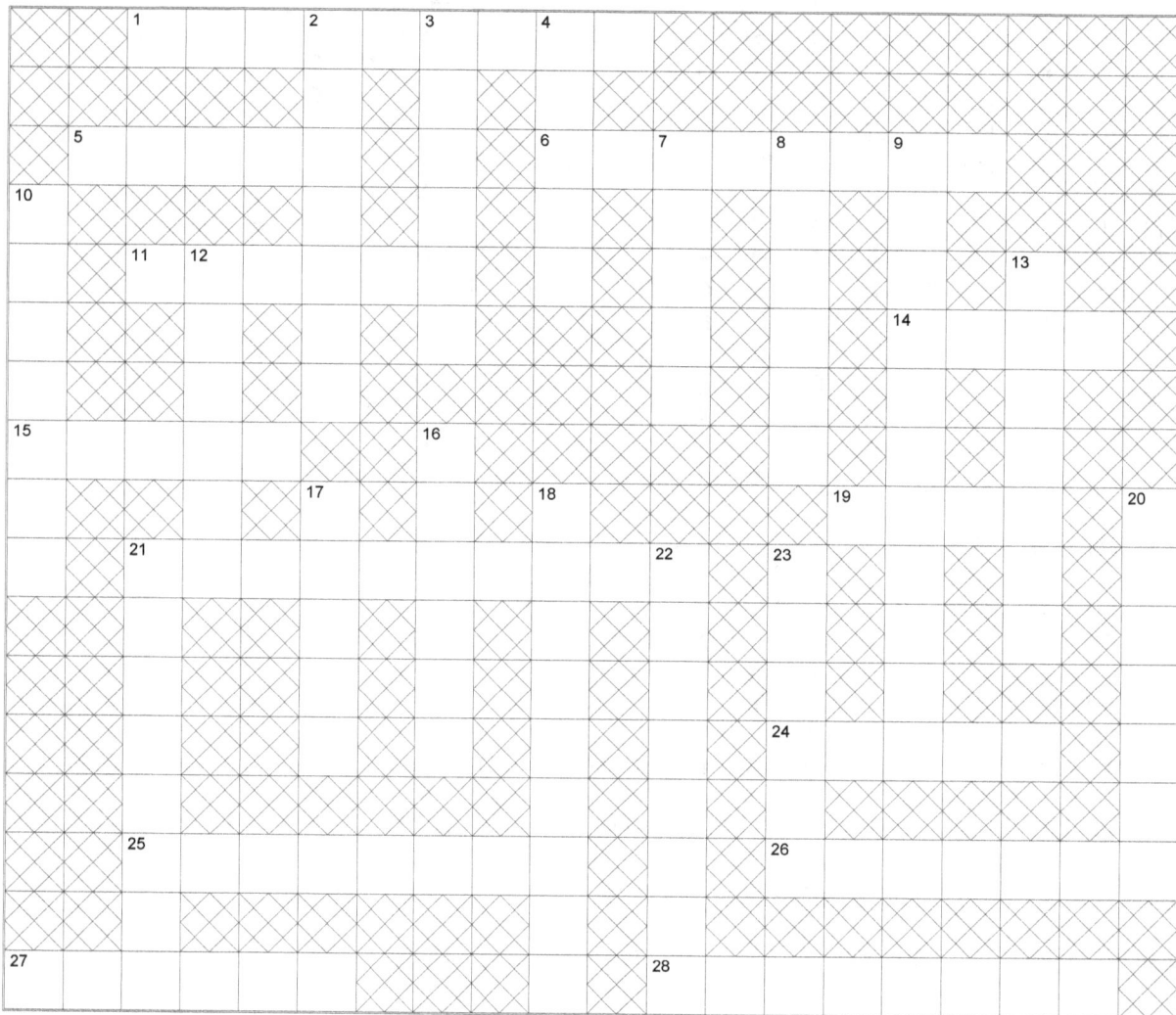

Across
1. Soothing; pacifying
5. Meeting arranged by lovers
6. Clear; understandable
11. Transmitter of prophecies at a shrine
14. Pile of things that can be used for burning corpses
15. Devastation; chaos
19. Disorderly retreat following a defeat
21. Funds donated to a group or individual
24. A wood nymph
25. The food of the gods, thought to give immortality
26. Worshiped as a god
27. Human-like creature with a goat's ears, horns, and legs
28. Marked by careful, persistent effort

Down
2. Lured; tempted
3. Gloomy; depressing
4. Female spirit that represents nature
7. Spirit that lives in brooks and springs
8. Of a son or a daughter
9. Lavishly; suggesting great expense
10. Embarrassed
12. Fame
13. A judge
16. Honor or respect that is shown publicly
17. A shaded, leafy recess or arbor
18. Given human form
20. Dirty from poverty or lack of care
21. Joyful; triumphant
22. Assisted; helped
23. Morally degraded

Mythology Vocabulary Crossword 1 Answer Key

		¹A	P	P	²E	A	³S	I	⁴N	G					
					N		O		Y						
		⁵T	R	Y	S	T		⁶M	⁷A	⁸N	I	⁹F	E	S	T
¹⁰A					I		B	P	A	I		U			
B		¹¹O	¹²R	A	C	L	E		H	I		L	M		¹³A
A			E		E		R			A	I	¹⁴P	Y	R	E
S			N		D					D	A	T		B	
¹⁵H	A	V	O	C		¹⁶H					L	U		I	
E			W	¹⁷B		O	¹⁸I			¹⁹R	O	U	T	²⁰S
D		²¹E	N	D	O	W	M	E	N	T	²²S	²³S	U	E	Q
		X		W		A		C			U		O	S	R	U
		U		E		G		A			C		R	L		A
		L		R		E		R			C	²⁴D	R	Y	A	D	L
		T						N			O	I				I
		²⁵A	M	B	R	O	S	I	A		R	²⁶D	E	I	F	I	E	D
		N						T			E				
²⁷S	A	T	Y	R	S			E		²⁸D	I	L	I	G	E	N	T

Across
1. Soothing; pacifying
5. Meeting arranged by lovers
6. Clear; understandable
11. Transmitter of prophecies at a shrine
14. Pile of things that can be used for burning corpses
15. Devastation; chaos
19. Disorderly retreat following a defeat
21. Funds donated to a group or individual
24. A wood nymph
25. The food of the gods, thought to give immortality
26. Worshiped as a god
27. Human-like creature with a goat's ears, horns, and legs
28. Marked by careful, persistent effort

Down
2. Lured; tempted
3. Gloomy; depressing
4. Female spirit that represents nature
7. Spirit that lives in brooks and springs
8. Of a son or a daughter
9. Lavishly; suggesting great expense
10. Embarrassed
12. Fame
13. A judge
16. Honor or respect that is shown publicly
17. A shaded, leafy recess or arbor
18. Given human form
20. Dirty from poverty or lack of care
21. Joyful; triumphant
22. Assisted; helped
23. Morally degraded

Mythology Vocabulary Crossword 2

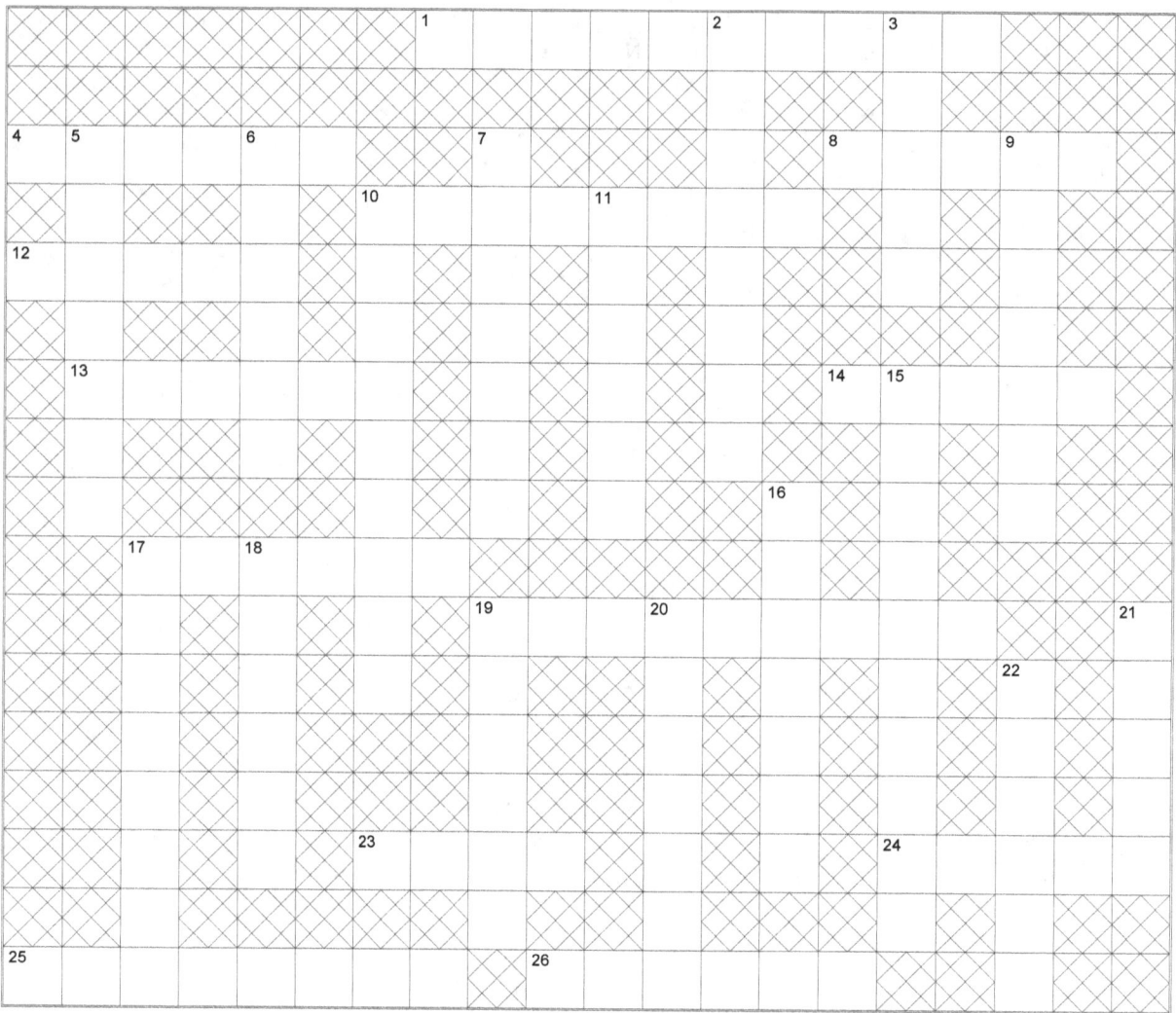

Across
1. Funds donated to a group or individual
4. Easily bent
8. Female spirit that represents nature
10. The food of the gods, thought to give immortality
12. Devastation; chaos
13. Honor or respect that is shown publicly
14. A shaded, leafy recess or arbor
17. Morally degraded
19. An original that serves as a model
23. Pile of things that can be used for burning corpses
24. Spirit that lives in brooks and springs
25. Balanced, rhythmic beats
26. Human-like creature with a goat's ears, horns, and legs

Down
2. Clear; understandable
3. Meeting arranged by lovers
5. Detested
6. Drink of the gods; undiluted juice of a fruit
7. Embarrassed
9. Sign; forewarning; omen
10. Soothing; pacifying
11. Transmitter of prophecies at a shrine
15. All-powerful
16. Lured; tempted
17. Assisted; helped
18. Fame
19. Trivial; lacking in importance
20. Turbulent or overwhelming flow
21. A wood nymph
22. Of a son or a daughter

Mythology Vocabulary Crossword 2 Answer Key

					1 E	N	D	O	W	2 M	E	N	3 T	S		
										A			R			
4 P	5 L	I	6 A	N	T		7 A			N		8 N	Y	9 M	P	H
	O		E			10 A	M	B	11 R	O	S	I	A		S		O
12 H	A	V	O	C		P		A		R		F			T		R
	T		T			P		S		A		E					T
	13 H	O	M	A	G	E		H		C		S		14 B	15 O	W	E	R
	E				R		A		L		T		M		N	
	D				S		D		E		16 E		N		T	
		17 S	18 O	R	D	I	D				N		I			
		U		E		N		19 P	R	20 O	T	O	T	Y	P	E		21 D
		C		N		G		A		T		I		O		22 F		R
		C		O				L		R		C		T		I		Y
		O		W				T		R		E		E		L		A
		R		N		23 P	Y	R	E		E		D		24 N	A	I	A	D
		E						Y			N				T		A	
25 C	A	D	E	N	C	E	S		26 S	A	T	Y	R	S		L	

Across
1. Funds donated to a group or individual
4. Easily bent
8. Female spirit that represents nature
10. The food of the gods, thought to give immortality
12. Devastation; chaos
13. Honor or respect that is shown publicly
14. A shaded, leafy recess or arbor
17. Morally degraded
19. An original that serves as a model
23. Pile of things that can be used for burning corpses
24. Spirit that lives in brooks and springs
25. Balanced, rhythmic beats
26. Human-like creature with a goat's ears, horns, and legs

Down
2. Clear; understandable
3. Meeting arranged by lovers
5. Detested
6. Drink of the gods; undiluted juice of a fruit
7. Embarrassed
9. Sign; forewarning; omen
10. Soothing; pacifying
11. Transmitter of prophecies at a shrine
15. All-powerful
16. Lured; tempted
17. Assisted; helped
18. Fame
19. Trivial; lacking in importance
20. Turbulent or overwhelming flow
21. A wood nymph
22. Of a son or a daughter

Mythology Vocabulary Crossword 3

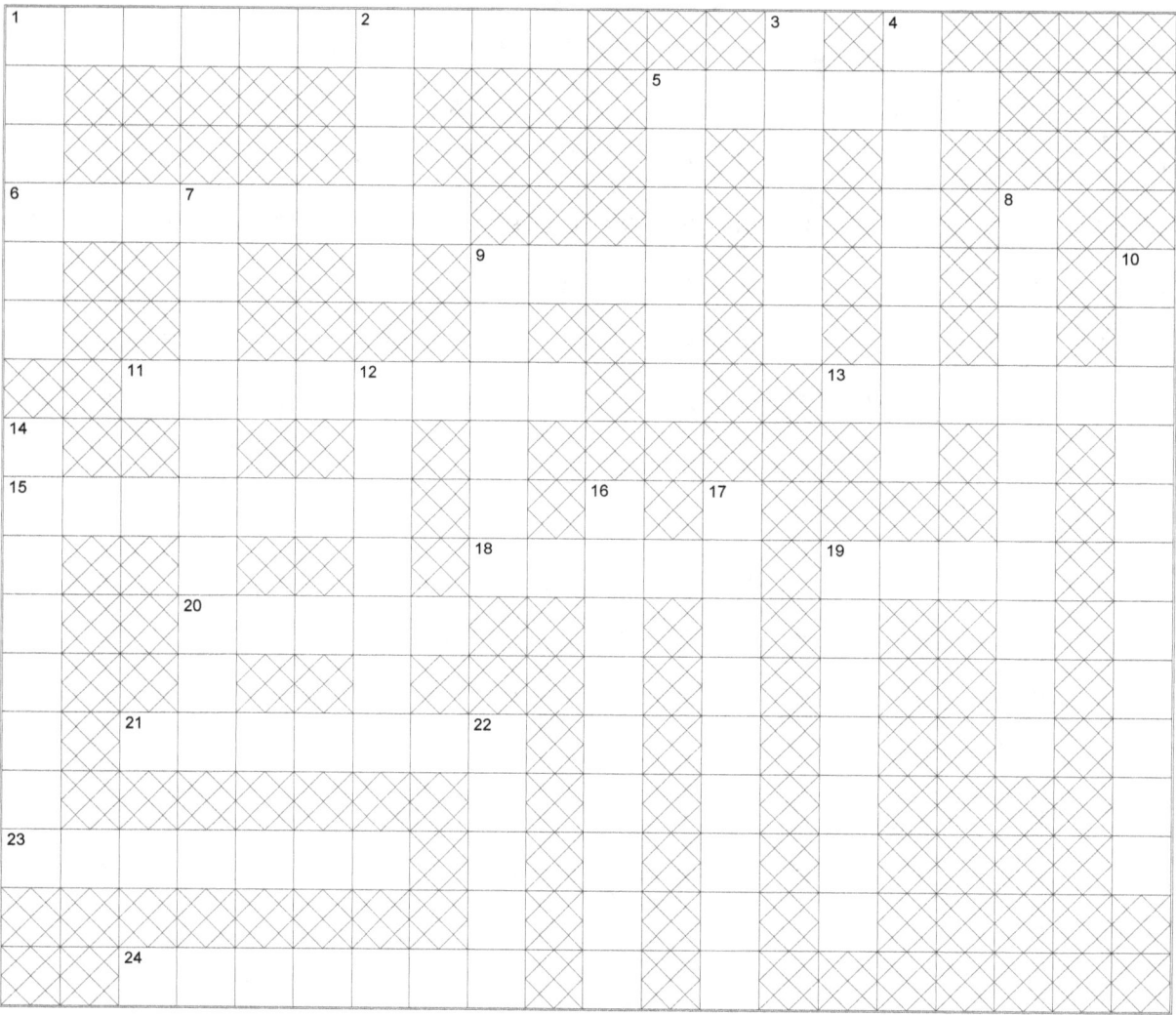

Across
1. Associating with
5. Easily bent
6. Clear; understandable
9. Disorderly retreat following a defeat
11. Joyful; triumphant
13. Drink of the gods; undiluted juice of a fruit
15. One who takes another's place by authority or force
18. Female spirit that represents nature
19. Pile of things that can be used for burning corpses
20. A shaded, leafy recess or arbor
21. Supposed to; considered to
23. Worshiped as a god
24. Straggler

Down
1. Loud expression of discontent
2. Meeting arranged by lovers
3. Of a son or a daughter
4. Inspired with love
5. Trivial; lacking in importance
7. Not able to be persuaded
8. Fatal epidemic disease
9. Fame
10. Lasting for an unlimited time
12. Turbulent or overwhelming flow
14. Assisted; helped
16. Outstanding; distinguished; of high quality
17. Embarrassed due to failure or disappointment
19. Person who has exceptional talents or powers
22. A wood nymph

Mythology Vocabulary Crossword 3 Answer Key

	1 C	O	N	S	O	2 R	T	I	N	G			3 F		4 E		
	L					R						5 P	L	I	A	N	T
	A					Y						A		L		A	
	6 M	A	7 I	F	E	S	T					L		I		M		8 P
	O		N			T			9 R	O	U	T		A		O			10 P
	R		E						E			R		L		13 N	E	C	T	A	R
			11 E	X	U	12 T	A	N	T			Y				N	E	C	T	A	R
	14 S		O			O			O							D		I		P
	15 U	S	U	R	P	E	R			16 W	E	17 C					L		E
	C		A						18 N	Y	M	P	H		19 P	Y	R	E		T
	C		20 B	O	W	E	R		I			A			R			N		U
	O		L			N			N			G			O			C		A
	R		21 R	E	P	U	T	E	22 D			R			D			E		L
	E								R			I			I					L
	23 D	E	I	F	I	E	D			Y			N			G					Y
									A			L			E					
			24 L	A	G	G	A	R	D			Y			D					

Across
1. Associating with
5. Easily bent
6. Clear; understandable
9. Disorderly retreat following a defeat
11. Joyful; triumphant
13. Drink of the gods; undiluted juice of a fruit
15. One who takes another's place by authority or force
18. Female spirit that represents nature
19. Pile of things that can be used for burning corpses
20. A shaded, leafy recess or arbor
21. Supposed to; considered to
23. Worshiped as a god
24. Straggler

Down
1. Loud expression of discontent
2. Meeting arranged by lovers
3. Of a son or a daughter
4. Inspired with love
5. Trivial; lacking in importance
7. Not able to be persuaded
8. Fatal epidemic disease
9. Fame
10. Lasting for an unlimited time
12. Turbulent or overwhelming flow
14. Assisted; helped
16. Outstanding; distinguished; of high quality
17. Embarrassed due to failure or disappointment
19. Person who has exceptional talents or powers
22. A wood nymph

Mythology Vocabulary Crossword 4

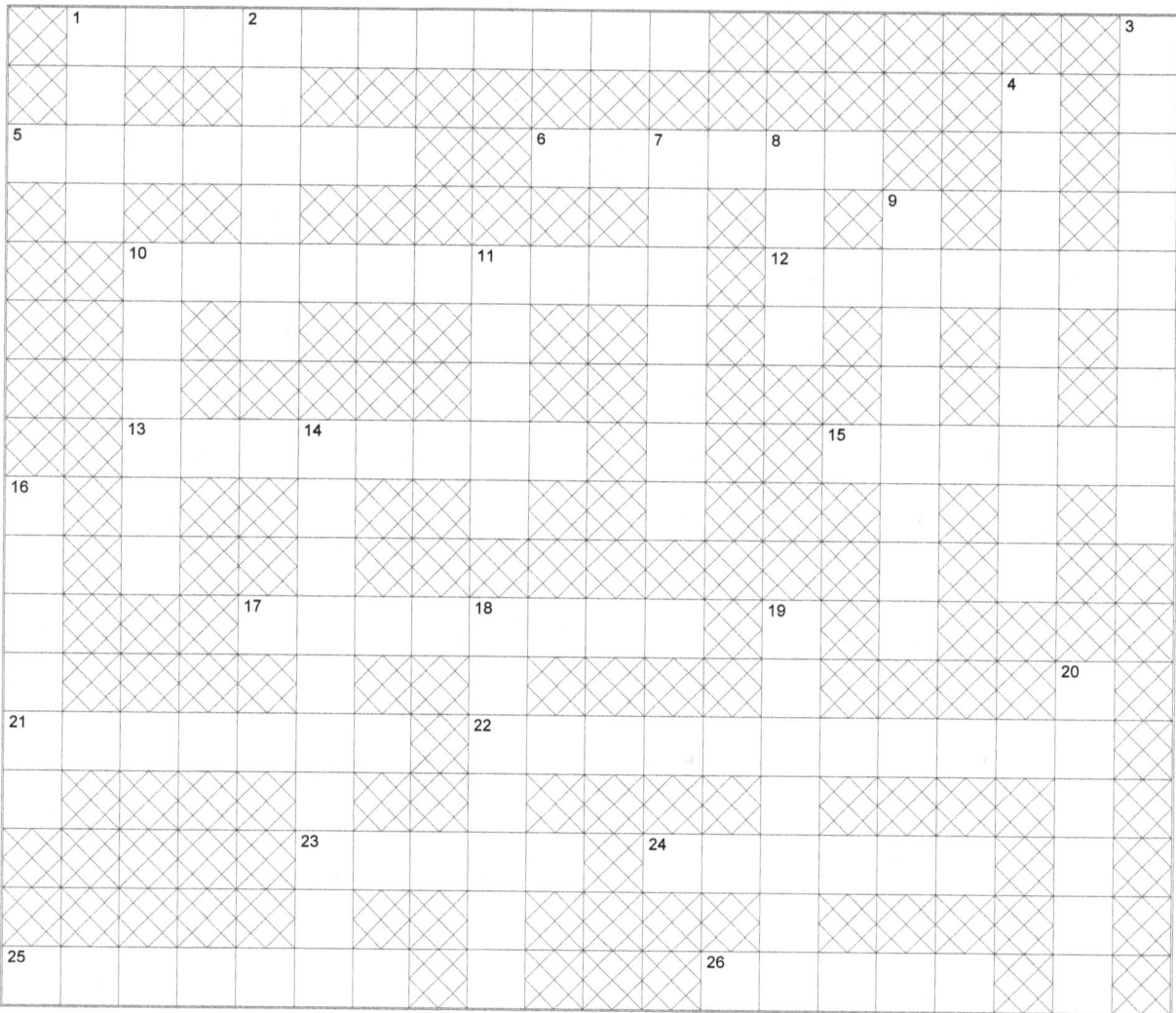

Across
1. Lasting for an unlimited time
5. Person who has exceptional talents or powers
6. Trivial; lacking in importance
10. Associating with
12. One who takes another's place by authority or force
13. Clear; understandable
15. Honor or respect that is shown publicly
17. Joyful; triumphant
21. Severe; having no decoration
22. Arousing fear or awe
23. A shaded, leafy recess or arbor
24. Human-like creature with a goat's ears, horns, and legs
25. Detested
26. A wood nymph

Down
1. Pile of things that can be used for burning corpses
2. Easily bent
3. Embarrassed due to failure or disappointment
4. Asking humbly
7. Straggler
8. Disorderly retreat following a defeat
9. Assisted; helped
10. Loud expression of discontent
11. Meeting arranged by lovers
14. Not able to be persuaded
16. Of a son or a daughter
18. Turbulent or overwhelming flow
19. A judge
20. Drink of the gods; undiluted juice of a fruit

Mythology Vocabulary Crossword 4 Answer Key

	1 P	E	R	2 P	E	T	U	A	L	L	Y					3 C
	Y			L										4 S		H
5 P	R	O	D	I	G	Y		6 P	7 A	L	8 T	R	Y		U		A
	E			A					A		O			9 S		P		G
			10 C	O	N	S	O	R	11 T	I	N	G		12 U	S	U	R	P	E	R
			L		T				R		Y			T		C		L		I
			A						Y							C		I		N
			13 M	A	14 N	I	F	E	S	T				15 H	O	M	A	G	E
16 F			O		I				T					R			N			D
I			R		E									E			T			
L					17 E	X	U	L	18 T	A	N	T		19 A		D			
I									O					R					20 N
21 A	U	S	T	E	R	E			22 R	E	D	O	U	B	T	A	B	L	E
L					A				R					I					C
					23 B	O	W	E	R			24 S	A	T	Y	R	S		T
					L				N			E							A
25 L	O	A	T	H	E	D			T			26 D	R	Y	A	D		R

Across

1. Lasting for an unlimited time
5. Person who has exceptional talents or powers
6. Trivial; lacking in importance
10. Associating with
12. One who takes another's place by authority or force
13. Clear; understandable
15. Honor or respect that is shown publicly
17. Joyful; triumphant
21. Severe; having no decoration
22. Arousing fear or awe
23. A shaded, leafy recess or arbor
24. Human-like creature with a goat's ears, horns, and legs
25. Detested
26. A wood nymph

Down

1. Pile of things that can be used for burning corpses
2. Easily bent
3. Embarrassed due to failure or disappointment
4. Asking humbly
7. Straggler
8. Disorderly retreat following a defeat
9. Assisted; helped
10. Loud expression of discontent
11. Meeting arranged by lovers
14. Not able to be persuaded
16. Of a son or a daughter
18. Turbulent or overwhelming flow
19. A judge
20. Drink of the gods; undiluted juice of a fruit

Mythology Vocabulary Juggle Letters 1

1. GTIANPIXE = 1. _____
   Making amends; atoning

2. TNICOMSNIE = 2. _____
   Knowing everything

3. AHMOEG = 3. _____
   Honor or respect that is shown publicly

4. RPTTNEO = 4. _____
   Sign; forewarning; omen

5. TIENENYLM = 5. _____
   Outstanding; distinguished; of high quality

6. OOARHTSESY = 6. _____
   A prophet

7. DOCIRUSLU = 7. _____
   Absurd; incongruous

8. MLRCAO = 8. _____
   Loud expression of discontent

9. BLMAEAILCP = 9. _____
   Not able to be appeased

10. ATYSRS = 10. _____
    Human-like creature with a goat's ears, horns, and legs

11. GRDAAGL = 11. _____
    Straggler

12. PTBCTNLOEEMI = 12. _____
    Despicable

13. LNPPSAIUT = 13. _____
    Asking humbly

14. UAACTIDY = 14. _____
    Daring; boldness

15. IDNESRICNG = 15. _____
    Distinguishing; perceiving as being different

Mythology Vocabulary Juggle Letters 1 Answer Key

1. GTIANPIXE = 1. EXPIATING
   Making amends; atoning

2. TNICOMSNIE = 2. OMNISCIENT
   Knowing everything

3. AHMOEG = 3. HOMAGE
   Honor or respect that is shown publicly

4. RPTTNEO = 4. PORTENT
   Sign; forewarning; omen

5. TIENENYLM = 5. EMINENTLY
   Outstanding; distinguished; of high quality

6. OOARHTSESY = 6. SOOTHSAYER
   A prophet

7. DOCIRUSLU = 7. LUDICROUS
   Absurd; incongruous

8. MLRCAO = 8. CLAMOR
   Loud expression of discontent

9. BLMAEAILCP = 9. IMPLACABLE
   Not able to be appeased

10. ATYSRS = 10. SATYRS
    Human-like creature with a goat's ears, horns, and legs

11. GRDAAGL = 11. LAGGARD
    Straggler

12. PTBCTNLOEEMI = 12. CONTEMPTIBLE
    Despicable

13. LNPPSAIUT = 13. SUPPLIANT
    Asking humbly

14. UAACTIDY = 14. AUDACITY
    Daring; boldness

15. IDNESRICNG = 15. DISCERNING
    Distinguishing; perceiving as being different

Mythology Vocabulary Juggle Letters 2

1. OYRETTPPO = 1. _____
   An original that serves as a model

2. ECITCUNMRV = 2. _____
   Go around or bypass

3. ELCIUALANLCB = 3. _____
   Unpredictability; impossible to foresee

4. INPTAL = 4. _____
   Easily bent

5. UUTSUSYMOPL = 5. _____
   Lavishly; suggesting great expense

6. ETUESRA = 6. _____
   Severe; having no decoration

7. YDCAUATI = 7. _____
   Daring; boldness

8. OUTRAISOLYC = 8. _____
   Horribly; cruelly

9. GAPPNESIA = 9. _____
   Soothing; pacifying

10. IDPORYG =10. _____
    Person who has exceptional talents or powers

11. ANDIA =11. _____
    Spirit that lives in brooks and springs

12. UYTFTILI =12. _____
    Frivolous; having no useful result

13. OAISARBM =13. _____
    The food of the gods, thought to give immortality

14. ITRABER =14. _____
    A judge

15. ITATACLUQ =15. _____
    A freeing or clearing from a charge or accusation

Mythology Vocabulary Juggle Letters 2 Answer Key

1. OYRETTPPO = 1. PROTOTYPE
   An original that serves as a model

2. ECITCUNMRV = 2. CIRCUMVENT
   Go around or bypass

3. ELCIUALANLCB = 3. INCALCULABLE
   Unpredictability; impossible to foresee

4. INPTAL = 4. PLIANT
   Easily bent

5. UUTSUSYMOPL = 5. SUMPTUOUSLY
   Lavishly; suggesting great expense

6. ETUESRA = 6. AUSTERE
   Severe; having no decoration

7. YDCAUATI = 7. AUDACITY
   Daring; boldness

8. OUTRAISOLYC = 8. ATROCIOUSLY
   Horribly; cruelly

9. GAPPNESIA = 9. APPEASING
   Soothing; pacifying

10. IDPORYG =10. PRODIGY
    Person who has exceptional talents or powers

11. ANDIA =11. NAIAD
    Spirit that lives in brooks and springs

12. UYTFTILI =12. FUTILITY
    Frivolous; having no useful result

13. OAISARBM =13. AMBROSIA
    The food of the gods, thought to give immortality

14. ITRABER =14. ARBITER
    A judge

15. ITATACLUQ =15. ACQUITTAL
    A freeing or clearing from a charge or accusation

Mythology Vocabulary Juggle Letters 3

1. PTRYOEOPT = 1. _____
   An original that serves as a model

2. AGFSUFER = 2. _____
   The right to vote

3. OESDRCCU = 3. _____
   Assisted; helped

4. PNNTIOMETO = 4. _____
   All-powerful

5. TPSUNIALP = 5. _____
   Asking humbly

6. LRACMO = 6. _____
   Loud expression of discontent

7. RYPATL = 7. _____
   Trivial; lacking in importance

8. EDANTPIRES = 8. _____
   Ordinary; not imaginative

9. UNILADIDFS = 9. _____
   Showing contempt

10. UTCDAYIA =10. _____
    Daring; boldness

11. OTGYYOHLM =11. _____
    Stories about the origin of a people, their gods, and heroes

12. EONRNW =12. _____
    Fame

13. ORNPYROOTM =13. _____
    High ridge of land that juts out into the water

14. SLIBEPETSCU =14. _____
    Easily affected or influenced

15. UIUOLSCDR =15. _____
    Absurd; incongruous

Mythology Vocabulary Juggle Letters 3 Answer Key

1. PTRYOEOPT = 1. PROTOTYPE
   An original that serves as a model

2. AGFSUFER = 2. SUFFRAGE
   The right to vote

3. OESDRCCU = 3. SUCCORED
   Assisted; helped

4. PNNTIOMETO = 4. OMNIPOTENT
   All-powerful

5. TPSUNIALP = 5. SUPPLIANT
   Asking humbly

6. LRACMO = 6. CLAMOR
   Loud expression of discontent

7. RYPATL = 7. PALTRY
   Trivial; lacking in importance

8. EDANTPIRES = 8. PEDESTRIAN
   Ordinary; not imaginative

9. UNILADIDFS = 9. DISDAINFUL
   Showing contempt

10. UTCDAYIA = 10. AUDACITY
    Daring; boldness

11. OTGYYOHLM = 11. MYTHOLOGY
    Stories about the origin of a people, their gods, and heroes

12. EONRNW = 12. RENOWN
    Fame

13. ORNPYROOTM = 13. PROMONTORY
    High ridge of land that juts out into the water

14. SLIBEPETSCU = 14. SUSCEPTIBLE
    Easily affected or influenced

15. UIUOLSCDR = 15. LUDICROUS
    Absurd; incongruous

Mythology Vocabulary Juggle Letters 4

1. MLAEETU = 1. _____
   Compete with successfully

2. GTIDINLE = 2. _____
   Marked by careful, persistent effort

3. YEIAEDVNRTTNL = 3. _____
   Accidentally

4. EUEPRTD = 4. _____
   Supposed to; considered to

5. LSSOOCUS = 5. _____
   A huge statue

6. BBELAETDRUO = 6. _____
   Arousing fear or awe

7. CSECUROD = 7. _____
   Assisted; helped

8. TNTENAEMO = 8. _____
   Making amends for an injury or wrong

9. TDTUSTIEE = 9. _____
   Impoverished; lacking means of subsistence

10. AGRGADL =10. _____
    Straggler

11. ORTETPN =11. _____
    Sign; forewarning; omen

12. RMIBOASA =12. _____
    The food of the gods, thought to give immortality

13. AEITFNMS =13. _____
    Clear; understandable

14. IOUACPCSRI =14. _____
    Impulsive; given to whim

15. BUTISLEPCSE =15. _____
    Easily affected or influenced

Mythology Vocabulary Juggle Letters 4 Answer Key

1. MLAEETU = 1. EMULATE
   Compete with successfully

2. GTIDINLE = 2. DILIGENT
   Marked by careful, persistent effort

3. YEIAEDVNRTTNL = 3. INADVERTENTLY
   Accidentally

4. EUEPRTD = 4. REPUTED
   Supposed to; considered to

5. LSSOOCUS = 5. COLOSSUS
   A huge statue

6. BBELAETDRUO = 6. REDOUBTABLE
   Arousing fear or awe

7. CSECUROD = 7. SUCCORED
   Assisted; helped

8. TNTENAEMO = 8. ATONEMENT
   Making amends for an injury or wrong

9. TDTUSTIEE = 9. DESTITUTE
   Impoverished; lacking means of subsistence

10. AGRGADL = 10. LAGGARD
    Straggler

11. ORTETPN = 11. PORTENT
    Sign; forewarning; omen

12. RMIBOASA = 12. AMBROSIA
    The food of the gods, thought to give immortality

13. AEITFNMS = 13. MANIFEST
    Clear; understandable

14. IOUACPCSRI = 14. CAPRICIOUS
    Impulsive; given to whim

15. BUTISLEPCSE = 15. SUSCEPTIBLE
    Easily affected or influenced

ABASHED	Embarrassed
ACQUIESCE	To consent without protest
ACQUITTAL	A freeing or clearing from a charge or accusation
AMBROSIA	The food of the gods, thought to give immortality
APPEASING	Soothing; pacifying
ARBITER	A judge

ASCRIBED	Attributed to
ATONEMENT	Making amends for an injury or wrong
ATROCIOUSLY	Horribly; cruelly
AUDACITY	Daring; boldness
AUSTERE	Severe; having no decoration
BOWER	A shaded, leafy recess or arbor

CADENCES	Balanced, rhythmic beats
CAPRICIOUS	Impulsive; given to whim
CHAGRINED	Embarrassed due to failure or disappointment
CIRCUMVENT	Go around or bypass
CLAMOR	Loud expression of discontent
COLOSSUS	A huge statue

CONSORTING	Associating with
CONTEMPTIBLE	Despicable
DAUNTLESS	Fearless; not intimidated
DEIFIED	Worshiped as a god
DESOLATE	Barren; lifeless
DESTITUTE	Impoverished; lacking means of subsistence

DILIGENT	Marked by careful, persistent effort
DISCERNING	Distinguishing; perceiving as being different
DISDAINFUL	Showing contempt
DIVINATION	The art of foretelling events by the use of the supernatural
DRYAD	A wood nymph
EMINENTLY	Outstanding; distinguished; of high quality

EMULATE	Compete with successfully
ENAMORED	Inspired with love
ENDOWMENTS	Funds donated to a group or individual
ENTICED	Lured; tempted
EXONERATE	Free from blame
EXPIATING	Making amends; atoning

EXULTANT	Joyful; triumphant
FILIAL	Of a son or a daughter
FUTILITY	Frivolous; having no useful result
HAVOC	Devastation; chaos
HOMAGE	Honor or respect that is shown publicly
IMPLACABLE	Not able to be appeased

INADVERTENTLY	Accidentally
INCALCULABLE	Unpredictability; impossible to foresee
INCARNATE	Given human form
INEVITABLE	Impossible to avoid
INEXORABLE	Not able to be persuaded
INFALLIBLY	Not capable of an error

LAGGARD	Straggler
LAMENTATION	A song or poem that expresses grief or mourning
LOATHED	Detested
LUDICROUS	Absurd; incongruous
MANIFEST	Clear; understandable
MYTHOLOGY	Stories about the origin of a people, their gods, and heroes

NAIAD	Spirit that lives in brooks and springs
NECTAR	Drink of the gods; undiluted juice of a fruit
NYMPH	Female spirit that represents nature
OMNIPOTENT	All-powerful
OMNISCIENT	Knowing everything
ORACLE	Transmitter of prophecies at a shrine

PALTRY	Trivial; lacking in importance
PEDESTRIAN	Ordinary; not imaginative
PERPETUALLY	Lasting for an unlimited time
PESTILENCE	Fatal epidemic disease
PLAUSIBLE	Having some truth, but open to doubt
PLIANT	Easily bent

PORTENT	Sign; forewarning; omen
PRODIGY	Person who has exceptional talents or powers
PROMONTORY	High ridge of land that juts out into the water
PROTOTYPE	An original that serves as a model
PYRE	Pile of things that can be used for burning corpses
RAIMENT	Clothing

REDOUBTABLE	Arousing fear or awe
RENOWN	Fame
REPUTED	Supposed to; considered to
RETINUE	Messengers; government representatives
ROUT	Disorderly retreat following a defeat
SATYRS	Human-like creature with a goat's ears, horns, and legs

SCUDDING	Skimming along swiftly and easily
SOMBER	Gloomy; depressing
SOOTHSAYER	A prophet
SORDID	Morally degraded
SQUALID	Dirty from poverty or lack of care
SUCCORED	Assisted; helped

SUFFRAGE	The right to vote
SUMPTUOUSLY	Lavishly; suggesting great expense
SUPPLIANT	Asking humbly
SUSCEPTIBLE	Easily affected or influenced
SUSTENANCE	The supporting of life or health
TORRENT	Turbulent or overwhelming flow

TRYST	Meeting arranged by lovers
UNFATHOMABLE	Not able to be understood
UNSULLIED	Not stained or tainted
USURPER	One who takes another's place by authority or force
VINDICTIVE	Unforgiving; seeking revenge

Mythology Vocabulary

LAMENTATION	PLIANT	EXULTANT	TORRENT	OMNIPOTENT
ATONEMENT	USURPER	SUFFRAGE	FUTILITY	SQUALID
DAUNTLESS	DISCERNING	FREE SPACE	ENDOWMENTS	CONTEMPTIBLE
ACQUITTAL	APPEASING	PROTOTYPE	AUSTERE	UNFATHOMABLE
PESTILENCE	DISDAINFUL	EMULATE	ATROCIOUSLY	SORDID

Mythology Vocabulary

SUPPLIANT	SOOTHSAYER	PROMONTORY	CIRCUMVENT	INFALLIBLY
CLAMOR	LOATHED	EMINENTLY	IMPLACABLE	ENAMORED
INCALCULABLE	ASCRIBED	FREE SPACE	SUSTENANCE	OMNISCIENT
PORTENT	REPUTED	INEXORABLE	HOMAGE	SUMPTUOUSLY
DESTITUTE	COLOSSUS	ROUT	ORACLE	AMBROSIA

Mythology Vocabulary

FILIAL	ENTICED	EMULATE	CHAGRINED	RENOWN
ROUT	OMNISCIENT	MANIFEST	CADENCES	DISDAINFUL
HAVOC	PESTILENCE	FREE SPACE	ENDOWMENTS	INEVITABLE
TORRENT	NECTAR	ASCRIBED	BOWER	INADVERTENTLY
SUFFRAGE	PORTENT	PROMONTORY	DESOLATE	ATONEMENT

Mythology Vocabulary

INFALLIBLY	AUDACITY	PROTOTYPE	IMPLACABLE	DILIGENT
ENAMORED	CAPRICIOUS	PLAUSIBLE	ORACLE	FUTILITY
RETINUE	DEIFIED	FREE SPACE	NYMPH	SOMBER
ACQUIESCE	SUSTENANCE	PRODIGY	VINDICTIVE	AMBROSIA
ATROCIOUSLY	EMINENTLY	RAIMENT	EXONERATE	DESTITUTE

Mythology Vocabulary

SUMPTUOUSLY	SATYRS	LAMENTATION	SUCCORED	NYMPH
SUSCEPTIBLE	PORTENT	SUPPLIANT	CAPRICIOUS	DIVINATION
CONSORTING	ABASHED	FREE SPACE	CONTEMPTIBLE	DAUNTLESS
ARBITER	AUDACITY	MYTHOLOGY	TRYST	HOMAGE
FUTILITY	AUSTERE	AMBROSIA	RENOWN	ENDOWMENTS

Mythology Vocabulary

EMINENTLY	CHAGRINED	LOATHED	EXONERATE	SOOTHSAYER
CADENCES	UNSULLIED	VINDICTIVE	INFALLIBLY	PLAUSIBLE
REDOUBTABLE	LUDICROUS	FREE SPACE	SQUALID	SOMBER
APPEASING	RETINUE	ATROCIOUSLY	DEIFIED	INCARNATE
ACQUIESCE	HAVOC	DILIGENT	USURPER	IMPLACABLE

Mythology Vocabulary

MYTHOLOGY	SUSTENANCE	ORACLE	AMBROSIA	DAUNTLESS
CIRCUMVENT	PLIANT	RENOWN	ENTICED	AUDACITY
ENAMORED	SUSCEPTIBLE	FREE SPACE	SORDID	ABASHED
ENDOWMENTS	DIVINATION	EMINENTLY	PLAUSIBLE	USURPER
NAIAD	UNFATHOMABLE	SUMPTUOUSLY	DISDAINFUL	DESTITUTE

Mythology Vocabulary

CADENCES	PERPETUALLY	DRYAD	SUCCORED	SOMBER
LOATHED	OMNIPOTENT	SUFFRAGE	ATONEMENT	HOMAGE
NECTAR	DESOLATE	FREE SPACE	NYMPH	PESTILENCE
INEVITABLE	TORRENT	ACQUITTAL	PEDESTRIAN	REDOUBTABLE
PROTOTYPE	ATROCIOUSLY	VINDICTIVE	CONSORTING	CONTEMPTIBLE

Mythology Vocabulary

ATROCIOUSLY	APPEASING	DESOLATE	LAMENTATION	MYTHOLOGY
PERPETUALLY	INEXORABLE	SUSCEPTIBLE	CIRCUMVENT	UNSULLIED
PESTILENCE	PROMONTORY	FREE SPACE	OMNIPOTENT	EMINENTLY
DESTITUTE	DISDAINFUL	DIVINATION	ENAMORED	ROUT
RENOWN	IMPLACABLE	PEDESTRIAN	FUTILITY	PLIANT

Mythology Vocabulary

HAVOC	EMULATE	AUSTERE	TORRENT	SUCCORED
ATONEMENT	CAPRICIOUS	SUPPLIANT	NYMPH	REPUTED
VINDICTIVE	EXPIATING	FREE SPACE	PALTRY	LUDICROUS
SUSTENANCE	ABASHED	SCUDDING	TRYST	DRYAD
INEVITABLE	DISCERNING	DILIGENT	ORACLE	DEIFIED

Mythology Vocabulary

CONSORTING	CLAMOR	OMNISCIENT	SUSCEPTIBLE	AMBROSIA
AUDACITY	VINDICTIVE	ARBITER	PALTRY	COLOSSUS
DEIFIED	DISCERNING	FREE SPACE	BOWER	INADVERTENTLY
REDOUBTABLE	RENOWN	CONTEMPTIBLE	PESTILENCE	USURPER
LOATHED	NECTAR	HAVOC	ACQUITTAL	DESTITUTE

Mythology Vocabulary

DISDAINFUL	ENTICED	SQUALID	ORACLE	INFALLIBLY
MYTHOLOGY	ASCRIBED	IMPLACABLE	FUTILITY	FILIAL
HOMAGE	UNFATHOMABLE	FREE SPACE	REPUTED	INEXORABLE
DESOLATE	SUCCORED	OMNIPOTENT	SORDID	SOOTHSAYER
APPEASING	PROMONTORY	INCALCULABLE	SUSTENANCE	SUPPLIANT

Mythology Vocabulary

REPUTED	LUDICROUS	BOWER	HOMAGE	INCARNATE
DILIGENT	ENTICED	INEXORABLE	UNFATHOMABLE	ATROCIOUSLY
SQUALID	AMBROSIA	FREE SPACE	EMULATE	UNSULLIED
INADVERTENTLY	CONSORTING	SATYRS	IMPLACABLE	SOOTHSAYER
ORACLE	COLOSSUS	SUSTENANCE	ACQUITTAL	LOATHED

Mythology Vocabulary

HAVOC	RETINUE	PYRE	DISCERNING	CHAGRINED
RAIMENT	PEDESTRIAN	ATONEMENT	SUMPTUOUSLY	ABASHED
CONTEMPTIBLE	DISDAINFUL	FREE SPACE	NYMPH	DESOLATE
EXPIATING	ASCRIBED	SUCCORED	VINDICTIVE	NAIAD
DESTITUTE	SOMBER	LAGGARD	PRODIGY	APPEASING

Mythology Vocabulary

CIRCUMVENT	ATONEMENT	ENTICED	OMNIPOTENT	CLAMOR
INCARNATE	COLOSSUS	SUSTENANCE	MYTHOLOGY	REPUTED
NYMPH	DAUNTLESS	FREE SPACE	ACQUITTAL	PORTENT
RAIMENT	TRYST	ABASHED	ENDOWMENTS	SCUDDING
USURPER	DILIGENT	PEDESTRIAN	REDOUBTABLE	RENOWN

Mythology Vocabulary

PROMONTORY	SOOTHSAYER	ASCRIBED	ROUT	PRODIGY
DIVINATION	SUPPLIANT	DESOLATE	ATROCIOUSLY	DISDAINFUL
FUTILITY	PERPETUALLY	FREE SPACE	CONTEMPTIBLE	ACQUIESCE
SOMBER	TORRENT	SORDID	CONSORTING	BOWER
SUFFRAGE	ENAMORED	SATYRS	INEXORABLE	CAPRICIOUS

Mythology Vocabulary

EXONERATE	TRYST	REPUTED	SATYRS	APPEASING
EXPIATING	PERPETUALLY	CHAGRINED	PLAUSIBLE	ROUT
ABASHED	ATONEMENT	FREE SPACE	UNSULLIED	DIVINATION
ACQUIESCE	UNFATHOMABLE	LAGGARD	PESTILENCE	PROMONTORY
ACQUITTAL	CIRCUMVENT	HAVOC	CONSORTING	SUMPTUOUSLY

Mythology Vocabulary

OMNIPOTENT	MYTHOLOGY	SUSCEPTIBLE	AMBROSIA	SUSTENANCE
CAPRICIOUS	DISDAINFUL	SORDID	INCALCULABLE	DISCERNING
PLIANT	LOATHED	FREE SPACE	ASCRIBED	DAUNTLESS
INEVITABLE	CADENCES	CLAMOR	ENDOWMENTS	RENOWN
NAIAD	EMINENTLY	SUCCORED	VINDICTIVE	DESTITUTE

Mythology Vocabulary

APPEASING	ACQUIESCE	SOOTHSAYER	INEXORABLE	USURPER
INADVERTENTLY	TORRENT	DESOLATE	CAPRICIOUS	LOATHED
PESTILENCE	RENOWN	FREE SPACE	SUMPTUOUSLY	INCALCULABLE
SCUDDING	NYMPH	DISCERNING	CONSORTING	DIVINATION
ACQUITTAL	BOWER	ATONEMENT	PALTRY	INEVITABLE

Mythology Vocabulary

PERPETUALLY	PROMONTORY	DEIFIED	SUFFRAGE	REPUTED
CHAGRINED	CADENCES	EMINENTLY	CIRCUMVENT	REDOUBTABLE
SQUALID	OMNISCIENT	FREE SPACE	CONTEMPTIBLE	MANIFEST
AUSTERE	AUDACITY	EMULATE	ENTICED	DILIGENT
ROUT	SOMBER	RETINUE	MYTHOLOGY	DESTITUTE

Mythology Vocabulary

DIVINATION	ACQUITTAL	APPEASING	AUSTERE	SUMPTUOUSLY
ENAMORED	CONSORTING	LOATHED	EMULATE	SOMBER
INADVERTENTLY	RAIMENT	FREE SPACE	CAPRICIOUS	PALTRY
ORACLE	CIRCUMVENT	EXULTANT	TORRENT	CONTEMPTIBLE
PRODIGY	LAGGARD	VINDICTIVE	INFALLIBLY	ROUT

Mythology Vocabulary

DRYAD	ATROCIOUSLY	PYRE	PLAUSIBLE	REPUTED
UNFATHOMABLE	CADENCES	DILIGENT	MYTHOLOGY	BOWER
EMINENTLY	PLIANT	FREE SPACE	SUSTENANCE	PROTOTYPE
ABASHED	EXPIATING	DISCERNING	NAIAD	COLOSSUS
SORDID	INCALCULABLE	PROMONTORY	PORTENT	PERPETUALLY

Mythology Vocabulary

EMULATE	PLIANT	MYTHOLOGY	PERPETUALLY	DESOLATE
SOOTHSAYER	SATYRS	ATONEMENT	PORTENT	TRYST
ENAMORED	CADENCES	FREE SPACE	NYMPH	INEXORABLE
DISCERNING	EXULTANT	EXONERATE	USURPER	CONTEMPTIBLE
AUDACITY	AUSTERE	FILIAL	INFALLIBLY	SUSCEPTIBLE

Mythology Vocabulary

ATROCIOUSLY	VINDICTIVE	MANIFEST	COLOSSUS	REPUTED
LAGGARD	INCARNATE	RETINUE	ACQUITTAL	ENTICED
SCUDDING	APPEASING	FREE SPACE	ROUT	LAMENTATION
PYRE	RAIMENT	SUPPLIANT	DESTITUTE	NAIAD
CONSORTING	EXPIATING	SOMBER	FUTILITY	PRODIGY

Mythology Vocabulary

CONSORTING	PESTILENCE	ACQUIESCE	NYMPH	PLAUSIBLE
TORRENT	DEIFIED	SORDID	MYTHOLOGY	PEDESTRIAN
UNFATHOMABLE	DAUNTLESS	FREE SPACE	ASCRIBED	FUTILITY
EMINENTLY	LAMENTATION	AUDACITY	PRODIGY	OMNIPOTENT
SATYRS	SQUALID	HOMAGE	DISCERNING	INADVERTENTLY

Mythology Vocabulary

CHAGRINED	EMULATE	EXULTANT	DILIGENT	CONTEMPTIBLE
COLOSSUS	ROUT	CAPRICIOUS	PALTRY	LUDICROUS
OMNISCIENT	RAIMENT	FREE SPACE	INCALCULABLE	PROTOTYPE
UNSULLIED	CLAMOR	APPEASING	SOMBER	DIVINATION
NECTAR	VINDICTIVE	ATROCIOUSLY	SUMPTUOUSLY	SUCCORED

Mythology Vocabulary

SUMPTUOUSLY	CLAMOR	CIRCUMVENT	LUDICROUS	NECTAR
HOMAGE	DISDAINFUL	ACQUIESCE	INEXORABLE	DAUNTLESS
PERPETUALLY	ROUT	FREE SPACE	PROMONTORY	FILIAL
UNSULLIED	ENDOWMENTS	AUDACITY	PYRE	PRODIGY
INCALCULABLE	TRYST	AUSTERE	DILIGENT	EXPIATING

Mythology Vocabulary

SUCCORED	LAGGARD	SUSTENANCE	INCARNATE	MYTHOLOGY
NAIAD	PALTRY	HAVOC	ATONEMENT	DISCERNING
TORRENT	INADVERTENTLY	FREE SPACE	CADENCES	SUFFRAGE
INFALLIBLY	ARBITER	REPUTED	SATYRS	SUPPLIANT
ACQUITTAL	PEDESTRIAN	UNFATHOMABLE	CONSORTING	ORACLE

Mythology Vocabulary

NAIAD	HOMAGE	ROUT	TRYST	RENOWN
UNFATHOMABLE	HAVOC	SQUALID	SUPPLIANT	PROTOTYPE
IMPLACABLE	PYRE	FREE SPACE	SUFFRAGE	EXPIATING
CIRCUMVENT	INCARNATE	INEVITABLE	INFALLIBLY	AMBROSIA
DAUNTLESS	PORTENT	LAMENTATION	OMNIPOTENT	RETINUE

Mythology Vocabulary

SCUDDING	SUCCORED	ENAMORED	SORDID	DISCERNING
INEXORABLE	VINDICTIVE	DESTITUTE	ENDOWMENTS	LOATHED
COLOSSUS	SATYRS	FREE SPACE	PLAUSIBLE	PLIANT
OMNISCIENT	ATROCIOUSLY	LAGGARD	CAPRICIOUS	EMINENTLY
ABASHED	DISDAINFUL	AUSTERE	REDOUBTABLE	DEIFIED

Mythology Vocabulary

PYRE	SUPPLIANT	SATYRS	CIRCUMVENT	DISDAINFUL
DISCERNING	EXPIATING	CHAGRINED	PERPETUALLY	DESTITUTE
APPEASING	EMINENTLY	FREE SPACE	LOATHED	INFALLIBLY
ENDOWMENTS	CADENCES	AUDACITY	REPUTED	LAMENTATION
VINDICTIVE	HOMAGE	RETINUE	PROTOTYPE	ASCRIBED

Mythology Vocabulary

ACQUIESCE	ENAMORED	ARBITER	SOOTHSAYER	NYMPH
DILIGENT	INEXORABLE	AUSTERE	USURPER	CAPRICIOUS
SCUDDING	ABASHED	FREE SPACE	INEVITABLE	NECTAR
ENTICED	PROMONTORY	CONSORTING	LAGGARD	PRODIGY
ROUT	PLAUSIBLE	DEIFIED	HAVOC	EXULTANT

www.ingramcontent.com/pod-product-compliance
Lightning Source LLC
Chambersburg PA
CBHW081452070526
44586CB00019B/2315